ROUTLEDGE LIBRARY EDITIONS: LIBRARY AND INFORMATION SCIENCE

Volume 45

IN THE SPIRIT OF 1992

IN THE SPIRIT OF 1992
Access to Western European Libraries and Literature

Edited by
MARY M. HUSTON AND MAUREEN PASTINE

LONDON AND NEW YORK

First published in 1992 by The Haworth Press, Inc.

This edition first published in 2020
by Routledge
2 Park Square, Milton Park, Abingdon, Oxon OX14 4RN

and by Routledge
52 Vanderbilt Avenue, New York, NY 10017

Routledge is an imprint of the Taylor & Francis Group, an informa business

© 1992 The Haworth Press, Inc.

All rights reserved. No part of this book may be reprinted or reproduced or utilised in any form or by any electronic, mechanical, or other means, now known or hereafter invented, including photocopying and recording, or in any information storage or retrieval system, without permission in writing from the publishers.

Trademark notice: Product or corporate names may be trademarks or registered trademarks, and are used only for identification and explanation without intent to infringe.

British Library Cataloguing in Publication Data
A catalogue record for this book is available from the British Library

ISBN: 978-0-367-34616-4 (Set)
ISBN: 978-0-429-34352-0 (Set) (ebk)
ISBN: 978-0-367-42298-1 (Volume 45) (hbk)
ISBN: 978-0-367-42300-1 (Volume 45) (pbk)
ISBN: 978-0-367-82333-7 (Volume 45) (ebk)

Publisher's Note
The publisher has gone to great lengths to ensure the quality of this reprint but points out that some imperfections in the original copies may be apparent.

Disclaimer
The publisher has made every effort to trace copyright holders and would welcome correspondence from those they have been unable to trace.

In the Spirit of 1992: Access to Western European Libraries and Literature

Mary M. Huston
Maureen Pastine
Editors

The Haworth Press, Inc.
New York • London

In the Spirit of 1992: Access to Western European Libraries and Literature has also been published as *The Reference Librarian*, Number 35, 1992.

© 1992 by The Haworth Press, Inc. All rights reserved. No part of this work may be reproduced or utilized in any form or by any means, electronic or mechanical, including photocopying, microfilm and recording, or by any information storage and retrieval system, without permission in writing from the publisher. Printed in the United States of America.

The Haworth Press, Inc. 10 Alice Street, Binghamton, NY 13904-1580 USA

Library of Congress Cataloging-in-Publication Data

In the spirit of 1992 : access to Western European libraries and literature / Mary M. Huston, Maureen Pastine, editors.
    p. cm.
    ". . . has also been published as the Reference librarian, number 35, 1992"—CIP t.p. verso.
    Includes bibliographical references.
    ISBN 1-56024-276-0 (acid-free paper)
    1. Library administration—Europe. 2. Information services and state—Europe. 3. Bibliography, National—Europe. 4. International librarianship. 5. Libraries and state—Europe. 6. Library cooperation—Europe. I. Huston, Mary M. II. Pastine, Maureen. III. Reference librarian.
Z678.8.E85156   1992
025.1'094—dc20
                                                             92-8730
                                                                   CIP

In the Spirit of 1992: Access to Western European Libraries and Literature

CONTENTS

Developments in Western European Library and Information Systems: An Introduction *Mary M. Huston*	1
ACTION PLANS AND SPECIAL INITIATIVES AMONG INTERNATIONAL LIBRARY BODIES	
Information Policy and Libraries in the European Community *Harold Dierickx*	5
1. Introduction	6
2. EC Information Policy and Some Derived Activities	6
3. Specific EC Activities for Libraries	18
4. Other Initiatives Towards Library Cooperation in Europe	26
5. Concluding Remarks	31
Cooperation Among Libraries in Europe: Current Realities, Future Prospects *Paula Goossens*	49
Requirements for Cooperation	50
Prospects for Cooperation in Europe	51
Cataloging Rules	52
Authority Data	52
Communication Standards	54
Systems Interconnection	54
Requirements for European Library Cooperation	55

NATIONAL DEVELOPMENT IN INFORMATION AND COMMUNICATION TECHNOLOGIES

Bibliographic Access in the United Kingdom: Some Current Factors   57
Philip Bryant

    The National Bibliographic Service   59

London and South Eastern Library Region (LASER)   71
J. M. Plaister

    Purposes   71
    History   73
    Organizational and Network Structure   74
    Database   74
    Hardware Configuration   75
    Telecommunications   76
    Software and File Structure   76
    Function and Services   76
    Cooperation with Other Systems, Data Exchange   78
    Costs of Development and Maintenance and Funds   79
    Members, Users of Network, Users Costs, Membership Fees, Users Instructions   79
    Future Plans   79
    Conclusions   81

Access to Information in the Nordic Countries   83
Antti Soini

    General Trends   83
    Denmark   84
    Finland   86
    Iceland   87
    Norway   88
    Sweden   90
    Co-Operation in Scandinavia   92

DEVELOPMENTS AND IMPLICATIONS OF ONLINE EUROPEAN DATABASES

Access to European Online Databases   **95**
    Erwin K. Welsch
    Eleanor Rodini
    Victoria Hill

Searching the FRANCIS Database	96
European Communities	105
The German National Bibliography on STN	110
Conclusions	117

1992 and Beyond: In Conclusion   **119**
    Maureen Pastine

Developments in Western European Library and Information Systems: An Introduction

Mary M. Huston

When officials of the European Community (EC) drew up the provisions of the Single European Act in 1985, setting in motion the move toward a fully integrated market by the end of 1992, they ignited a quiet revolution. While it may not be completely realized by the end of 1992, a unified economic market without internal borders is assured, and the member countries of the EC are now envisioning the possibility of a single European currency, a central bank, and a political union.

As a political entity, the European Community consists of twelve member countries: Belgium, Denmark, France, Germany, Greece, Ireland, Italy, Luxembourg, the Netherlands, Portugal, Spain, and the United Kingdom. Other countries in both Western and Eastern Europe are now requesting membership, causing some observers to speak seriously of a future United States of Europe.

The Single European Act has had another, unintended consequence: it has stimulated the emergence of unprecedented cooperation among professionals both within and across national borders. The resulting machine-readable, increasingly linked knowledge databases promise to irrevocably change international research. Unfortunately, despite the importance of these developments, awareness of Western European information sources is not widespread among American readers, nor even among generalist information specialists; "the perspective of the reference/information world is limited" (Katz, 1987, 1).

© 1992 by The Haworth Press, Inc. All rights reserved.

For this reason, distinguished European library leaders have been invited to discuss key initiatives among their information communities in this special issue. In turn, Western European specialists in the United States have been selected to discuss other special topics critical to contemporary information provision on Western Europe. These contributions will provide descriptions of present and projected achievements in bibliographic control and bibliographic services, offering both means and methods of electronically mining Western European resources from this side of the Atlantic.

Leading the list of contributors is Harold Dierickx, Head of the Library Liaison Division of the European Parliament in Luxembourg and Chairman of EUROLIB (European Community and Associated Institutions Library Cooperative Group). From his position in an EC administrative institution, Mr. Dierickx provides a contextual introduction to the Western European information environment. Within that framework, he discusses the emerging EC information policy, highlighting its support of modern information technology and information services markets intended to establish comprehensive bibliographic control and library and document delivery services (EUROLIB) for European integration.

His is one of several organizations operating at various levels and interacting with each other to develop and integrate library and information systems. Therefore, he reviews as well the roles of other agencies in this sector, including the Council of Europe, the League des Bibliotheques Européennes de Recherche (LIBER), the Online Library Computer Systems (OCLC), and the European Foundation for Library Cooperation, in terms of their contributions to intra-European economic development.

The theme of the interinstitutional cooperative among members of the European library community has been developed as well by Paula Goossens of the Koninklijke Bibliotheek Albert I, Brussels, Belgium. Ms. Goossens reviews past, present, and future cooperative access strategies for sharing the resources of individual collections across geopolitical boundaries. She reviews efforts to enhance access through international cooperation in establishing cataloging rules, authority data, communication standards, and systems interconnectivity.

In his position as Director of the Centre for Bibliographic Management and the UK Office for Library Networking, Philip Bryant enjoys a unique bifocular vision of both national (UK) and international developments. From that perspective, he discusses the state of bibliographic access in the United Kingdom within the framework of the European Commission's "Plan of Action for Libraries in the EC." The national bibliographic service, bibliographic standards and the book trade, and the bourgeoning networking traffic are major foci of his illuminating review.

Having first read Bryant's overview on the state of affairs in the United Kingdom, the next contribution in this section of the issue focuses on a specific British organization for library cooperation. J. M. Plaister, Director of the London and South Eastern Library Region (LASER), illustrates the possibilities of employing human cooperation and communication and information technology to make economic and multiple use of regional bibliographic records and documents.

From their position north of the European continent, three (Finland, Norway, and Sweden) of the four Nordic countries (Denmark being the exception) are unaffiliated with the EC (at this time, though there are indications that one or more may soon affiliate with the EC). Regardless, the Nordic countries have made significant progress individually and collectively in achieving a "Union Nordic Library." Antti Soini, Director of the Automation Unit of Finnish Research Libraries, describes the national services and databases developed out of this long tradition of cooperation in Scandinavia.

Lastly, on this side of the Atlantic, three subject specialists from the University of Wisconsin-Madison describe access to European online databases and their capabilities. Erwin Welsch, Eleanor Rodini, and Victoria Hill discuss FRANCIS, a French database for the humanities, the European Communities Databases, and the German national bibliography.

And what are the implications for such developments? That is the subject of Maureen Pastine's concluding essay.

These contributions anticipate a heightened interest in Western Europe, as the European Community becomes a reality in 1992.

These contributors have in common a commitment to forge strategies which will increase access to an impressive bank of European databases by an expanded global clientele, thereby furthering the collapse of access boundaries. More ambitiously, this issue hopes to further information exchange among Europeans and Americans. We can only speculate on the progress which could result from forging new human and technological partnerships through enhanced information exchange.

BIBLIOGRAPHY

Katz, Bill. "Introduction: The World of Reference and Information Services." In International Aspects of Reference and Information Services, edited by Bill Katz and Ruth A. Fraley, page 1. New York: The Haworth Press, Inc. 1987.

ACTION PLANS AND SPECIAL INITIATIVES AMONG INTERNATIONAL LIBRARY BODIES

Information Policy and Libraries in the European Community

Harold Dierickx

SUMMARY. In the first section an attempt is made to identify what may be called an EC information policy formulated as such and translated into a number of programmes and activities mainly by the Commission. A following section surveys some EC activities specifically directed at libraries. Some initiatives in support of library promotion and cooperation within the wider European framework (i.e., not originated by EC institutions) are also mentioned. Some personal observations follow these descriptive sections. Finally some practical suggestions for accessing EC information are given in annex.

Harold Dierickx is Directorate-General for Research, European Parliament, Luxembourg. He holds graduate and post-graduate degrees in economics, international relations and library and information science.

Responsibility for this article is entirely that of the author. Nothing contained therein should be interpreted as a formal opinion or commitment on behalf of the European Communities in general, the European Parliament or EUROLIB in particular.

© 1992 by The Haworth Press, Inc. All rights reserved.

1. INTRODUCTION

The general theme of this issue is "Access to Western European Libraries and Literature." The purpose of this article is to highlight, within that general theme, a number of pertinent activities in the field of library and information policy by the European Community (EC) and its institutions. As a political entity, the EC is composed of twelve member countries: Belgium, Denmark, France, Germany, Greece, Ireland, Italy, Luxembourg, the Netherlands, Portugal, Spain and the United Kingdom. The main institutions that jointly administer the cooperation between these countries are: the Commission of the European Communities (CEC), the Council of Ministers, the Court of Auditors, the Court of Justice, the Economic and Social Committee, the European Investment Bank, the European Parliament. It should be noted that, in this article, the expression "European Community" (EC) refers to the joint territory occupied by the twelve Member States whereas the expression "European Communities" or "EC institutions" refers to the administering institutions mentioned above.

The present article makes no pretension to comprehensiveness. The entire field of EC information and information policy is so vast and complex that, within the limited space of an article, only a few salient points and some major directions can be indicated.

2. EC INFORMATION POLICY AND SOME DERIVED ACTIVITIES

As already pointed out in the Introduction, EC activities specifically concerning libraries are dealt with in a separate section.

2.1 Is There an EC Information Policy?

MALLEY states categorically "There is no EEC information policy at present . . ."[1] Perhaps he comes to this conclusion because of his broad definition of information policy as "policy directed by government to co-ordinate all matters concerning the organization and dissemination of information"[2] and his general view that information policy tends to be subsumed within wider, market-driven and commercially oriented policies,[3] a view shared by CUNNINGHAM, specifically with regard to EC information policy.[4]

Even if Malley's broad definition of information policy is accepted, the present author is of the opinion that an EC information policy definitely exists although it is not usually labelled as such and, indeed, is often part of broader or other policies or activities.

The driving factor behind the emergence of an EC information policy is the fear of Europe being totally dominated by Japanese and US competition in the information market. This is evident from writings dealing directly or indirectly with the European information industry and related policies. A quick glance at some figures explains the concern:

In 1981 the European online information market had an estimated turnover of 185.7 million US dollars against 680 million US dollars for the US. At the same time US suppliers accounted for 50 per cent of the scientific and technical information section of the online market in Europe.[5] In 1985 the global market size for the online information industry was estimated to be 5 billion US dollars, of which 4,150 million US dollars in the USA, 310 million US dollars in Japan, 200 million US dollars in the UK, 105 million US dollars in Germany, 65 million US dollars in France and 170 million US dollars in the rest of the world.[6] Europe's share in this was about 10 per cent (within this, 7.5 per cent taken up by the three countries mentioned). Of the 2,901 databases existing at the end of 1985, 76 per cent were North American, 17 per cent European and 7 per cent were located elsewhere.

Another worrying factor for Europe is its fundamental weakness in information technology in general. With the exception of telecommunications equipment, Western Europe has large trade deficits in computing, consumer electronics and components. Over 50 per cent of the European telecommunications industry's needs in integrated circuits are imported.[7]

The above figures may or may not be controversial and do not go beyond 1985. In any case they explain Europe's concern with its international competitive position as regards the information industry.

A good summary of the basic preoccupations, philosophy and

objectives underlying EC information policy is given in an article by Van Rosendaal.[5] After comparing the US and European online information industry in 1981 (see above), he points out the reasons for the success of the United States and Japan in the information industry:

- relatively large and homogeneous domestic markets which give economies of scale;
- start-up stimulation by government in combination with industry;
- favourable environment and market conditions for private enterprise.

It is only fair to say that the EC information policy and the derived activities have aimed at emulating these US and Japanese conditions in the face of the fragmented European market due to many barriers such as different languages, different copyright laws, different government practices in production and dissemination of information, different ways of operating national telecommunications monopolies.

Van Rosendaal also points at the social and cultural value of information, in addition to being an economic product or service, as being particularly relevant for the European Community with its different languages and cultures, but he emphasizes that attitudes which are economically unfavourable should be avoided. The same preoccupation with the social, cultural and political (in the sense of democracy and power-sharing) dimensions of information is also reflected in a publication based on the proceedings of an early conference on the theme "Information technology: Impact on Representation and Sharing of Power[8]", organized within the framework of the EC's FAST programme (see below). In reality, however, EC information policy and the ensuing programmes are mainly focusing on the introduction of advanced information technology and free market conditions.

Some concrete policy measures and activities are briefly described in the following sections.

2.2 The FAST Programme

FAST (Forecasting and Assessment in the field of Science and Technology) was implemented early in 1979 following a decision in 1978 by the EC Council of Ministers. The original aim of this five-year programme was to study all vital questions of Europe's existence and future, including economic, social, political, technological and environmental issues. Eventually, only the objective of defining a coherent science and technology policy for Europe was retained. Part of this reduced objective was to redefine as well existing economic and social policies. One main area of concern to FAST was the study of progress towards a "European information society." Five strategic issues were defined in this context: (1) Europe's position in key information technology; (2) Europe's position in the emerging international information and communication system; (3) the question of alienation versus integration within the information society; (4) implications for employment; (5) education and training. In particular the first two considerations were given priority attention in subsequent EC programmes.

Follow-up programmes, i.e., FAST II (1984-1987) and FAST III (current) continue to study the anticipated developments of science and technology and their impact on the economic and social evolution.[9]

2.3 The Framework Programmes

These embody EC research and development activities in the field of science and technology: they set objectives and determine EC financial contributions towards the various activities within the programme.[10] The second (current) Framework Programme covers the period 1987-1991 and has a total allocation of 5,396 million ECU[11], which is equivalent to about 3 per cent of the total Ec budget and 2 per cent of the combined research and development budgets of the Member States. Of this amount, 2,275 million ECU is earmarked under the heading "Towards a large market and an information and communications society" as follows:

- Information technologies: 1,600 million ECU
- Telecommunications: 550 million ECU
- New services of common interest (including transport): 125 million ECU

The specific programme concerned with information technology is ESPRIT (European strategic programme for research and development in information technologies). In this strategic sector, it is estimated that the EC covers only 10 per cent of the world market and barely 30 per cent of its own market; it had a trade deficit of about 15 billion ECU in electronics in 1986. ESPRIT aims at coordinating and stimulating European research in the pre-competitive stage by associating laboratories from universities, companies and research institutions. Each project is financed for 50 per cent by the EC and must include at least two different and independent companies from two different Member States.

ESPRIT I (1984-1987) had a budget of 750 million ECU; ESPRIT II (1988-1991) has a budget of 1,600 million ECU. ESPRIT II's priorities are micro electronics and peripherals, information processing systems and the development of application-specific integrated circuits. ESPRIT has been generally recognized as very successful.[12,13,14,15] Among other things it has fostered standardization, one of the means to do away with fragmentation of the European market, it has promoted cooperation among European firms and has helped them to meet competition from the US and Japan.

Other EC programmes that may be mentioned as part of the current Framework Programme are:[10,16]

- RACE (Research and development in advanced communications technologies in Europe):

   RACE's objective is the Community-wide introduction of Integrated Broadband Communications (IBC) by 1995, taking into account the evolving ISDN (Integrated Services Digital Network) and national introduction strategies. This should allow digital transmission of data, images and voice. The EC finances RACE projects for 50 per cent in partnership with industry and telecommunications operators. A budget of 550 million ECU is foreseen for 1987-1991.

- Information technology application programmes:

  - AIM: Advanced Informatics in Medicine in Europe (20 million ECU for an initial pilot phase of eighteen months).
  - DELTA: Developing European Learning through Technological Advance (20 million ECU for 1988-1990).
  - DRIVE: Dedicated Road Infrastructure for Vehicle Safety in Europe (60 million ECU for 1988-1991).

2.4 Introduction of the Integrated Services Digital Network (ISDN)

Within the world-wide framework conceived for ISDN by the CCITT (The International Telephone and Telegraph Consultative Committee of the International Telecommunications Union), the EC is promoting ISDN in Europe by a number of regulatory instruments.[17,18]

The ISDN can be considered as a natural evolution of the telephone network which will allow, via a single access, using the existing telephone subscriber line, the transmission of voice (telephony), text, data and images in the form of a multitude of more efficient or new services. ISDN will pave the way for the introduction of Integrated Broadband Communications (IBC), the objective of the RACE programme. In the 1989 progress report on the introduction of ISDN in Europe,[19] the Commission states that because of progress made during 1989 on standardization, study of the application of the Open Network Provision (ONP) concept to ISDN (elimination of intra-European technical, tariff and legal barriers) and plans for drawing up specifications for procurement of ISDN terminals, a full pan-European ISDN service can be expected to be available by 1992. It adds that it will be critical for the eventual success of the common efforts undertaken so far to develop and implement clearly defined marketing and tariff strategies and promote a common social perception of this new medium.

The Commission clearly sees the introduction of an open ISDN in Europe as a corner-stone of its policy to create an integrated European market and, in particular, a barrier-free information services market. ISDN should provide business, in particular small businesses, and the private household with access to the new services that are to be built on it in accordance with free user choice and demand. ISDN is expected to provide the vital infrastructure for information-related and communication services for the business sector, with 85 per cent of total value-added services revenues projected for 1990 to relate to credit, financial, economic and marketing information and to financial transactions.[20]

2.5 The Interinstitutional Integrated Services Information System INSIS

The current INSIS programme is considered as the pilot phase of an EC interinstitutional integrated information system for the exchange of information between the EC institutions and the Member States administrations[21] using equipment and systems incorporating advanced information and communications technologies.

The current phase, in principle ending in 1990, concentrates on the following areas:[22]

1. electronic data transmission (transmission of documents, electronic mail, file transmission, video transmission);
2. access to EC information;
3. video conferencing.

It appears to this author that the most notable success of INSIS is the introduction of an electronic mail system, including EC institutions and some counterpart offices in Member States, and of a video conferencing facility for the EC institutions, mainly used by officials from the Commission and the European Parliament. Access to the various sources of information is still not standardized and, therefore, a complicated business for most users.

In connection with improving access to EC databases it should be mentioned though that INSIS is financing a project called "Simplification of Access to Information using Normalized Transfer" (SAINT) which has produced a state-of-the-art report[23] on (a) advanced querying and retrieval techniques which support users in accessing information in various sorts of information systems and (b) the data communications infrastructure which supports this information access. As to the latter, the study suggested a concrete approach for the lower layers of the OSI[24] communication model:

- definition of a remote database access system, using X.400 connectionless and transactional modes of communication;
- basing the system on existing, well-established tools within the UNIX environment, in particular TCP/IP protocols.

As to advanced querying and retrieval techniques, the competent services of the Commission have subcontracted concrete development work for intelligent interfaces.

INSIS has so far been much more a research and development funding organism than an information system. There is still a long way to go before reaching the Community-wide interinstitutional integrated information system envisaged by the 1982 Council decision. However, a "strategic study" is now under way which is to review past activities and achievements and to make recommendations for future development. At the time of writing only a draft interim report was available from which it appears inter alia that, in the future, INSIS should focus more on the practical application of commercially available information technology than on stimulating development of new technology, aim at closer involvement of users in policy-formulation and programme-management, and pay more attention to marketing and distributing its products and services as well as to timely delivery.

2.6 The Creation of a European Information Services Market

The programmes referred to above emphasized information technology rather than the provision of information itself. Since 1984,[25] however, the EC has given increasing attention to the creation of an EC information services market as one of the vital components of its policy directed at the creation of a free internal market of services and goods by the end of 1992.[26]

Before turning to these latest initiatives, some earlier Community action to create a free information market in EC Europe should be mentioned.

In 1980 the Commission launched the Euronet/DIANE network,

the first transnational packet-switched network in Europe, which supported multiple public and private online information databases and which charged distance-independent tariffs throughout Europe. Euronet operated successfully until 31 December 1984 when it was phased out as a physical network to be replaced by a system of various interconnections between the packet-switched networks meanwhile introduced and administered by the national PTTs (post, telegraph and telecommunications administrations). Whereas the databases being made available throughout Europe in this way have constantly been increasing, problems of technical incompatibility and large variations in charges for transborder data flows have arisen. This situation is now improving because of the emerging EC telecommunications policy[27] which clearly aims at the creation of a common market in telecommunications services and equipment and at reducing to a minimum the monopolies of the national telecommunications administrations. Two recent directives limit national telecommunications' monopolies to control of the basic network and voice telephony and guarantee right of access to the national networks for value-added information services by independent suppliers. Principles for harmonizing technical interfaces, conditions for supply and usage of services and proposals for harmonized tariff principles are included in the directives.[28] It does not look as if the EC telecommunications market is as free as that of the US but it is certainly moving in that direction. Persistent barriers that are still reducing the advantages — for example — of computerized international book trade systems are inter alia prohibitive costs of international telecommunications tariffs, taxes and postal rates.[29]

ECHO is the EC host which provides access to Community databases including ECLAS, the database of the Central Library of the Commission. It also hosts temporarily some new databases that are launched in Europe.

Other earlier EC initiatives that may be mentioned in the present context are DOCDEL, a programme of studies concerned with document delivery including experiments in online ordering, delivery by satellite link, by fax and from optical discs. SYSTRAN is the Commission's automatic translation system (still under development).

EUROTRA is a study programme in the field of machine translation sponsored by the EC. The Commission also publishes the free bi-monthly newsletter "I'M—Information Market" which is an ongoing source of information on the EC information market and the Commission's related activities.

The Commission's more recent activities in support of the EC information market are carried out under the so-called IMPACT programme ("Information Market Policy Actions"). The plan of action which was defined in the annex to the above mentioned Council Decision[26] is known as IMPACT-1, covers the period 1989-1990 and was given a budget of 36 million ECU for these two years. The main components of the plan are:

(1) Establishment of a European Information Market Observatory: The purpose of this activity is to improve the quality, reliability and availability of statistics on the information industry. To this end a secretariat has been established within the Commission that, in close collaboration with experts in Member States, commissions the collection of such statistics as well as conceptual studies in the field.

(2) Overcoming Technical, Administrative and Legal Barriers: In conformity with the Council decision the Commission has set up a Legal Advisory Board[30] composed of legal experts from Member States, to advise on legal issues relating to the information industry. During its regular meetings the Board gives priority to issues such as intellectual property, authentication of electronic signatures, computer fraud, liability in relation to information services, confidentiality of database searches and protection of privacy.

Under the same heading the Commission, in consultation with information providers and users, is exploring the possibilities for agreement on simplification and standardization of access to database services. It is planning to adopt the latest version of the ISO Command Language[31] for its own database services and has commissioned the development of a number of intellectual interfaces, including MITI. The latter is an advanced multilingual intelligent interface which will enable untrained users to have access to different databases on a number of different hosts in a uniform way, using natural language. The interface will include guidance on database selection, automatic construction of Boolean Search statements, transparent connection to hosts and search guidance through knowledge-based rules.[32]

(3) Improvement of the Synergy Between the Public and the Private Sectors: The Commission has published a set of recommendations[33] aiming at defining the respective roles of the public and private sectors in the production and distribution of information services. One of the basic objectives is that the public sector should only provide information services directly to the public when the private sector is unable or unwilling to do so. Public sector activity should in any case not lead to unfair competition and should in general be geared to support the private information industry. Value-added exploitation by the private sector of information generated by the public sector should be encouraged. The guidelines which are advisory only have been drafted in consultation with representatives of the public and private sectors of the European information market in all EC Member States.

(4) Pilot/Demonstration Projects: Under this IMPACT heading, in order to enlarge and stimulate the information market, the Commission provides partial support for a number of projects which demonstrate innovative applications of technology in new areas of information supply. One of the criteria of acceptance is that partners from several Member States are involved in any one project. This component of the IMPACT-1 programme is the largest with a budget of 23 million ECU. By April 1990 the Commission had approved 11 projects representing a total investment of 45 million ECU to which it was contributing 13 million ECU.[34] The projects cover the respective areas of patent tourism and geographical information as well as intelligent interfaces (e.g., see MITI above). The TECDOC project allows consultation of car repair and parts catalogues on CD-ROM equipment. Wherever possible these projects promote the use of common standards. Some of the projects combine several media such as still and moving images, text and sound.

(5) Promotion of the Use of European Information Services: This activity is meant to assist private sector information providers and Member States, mainly by providing information about services available and by giving initial support to new entrants into the mar-

ket. ECHO, the Commission's own host, is the main vehicle. The databases and databanks offered by ECHO are multilingual, mainly of a European nature, and range from information on research projects, research reports, research organizations and a multilingual terminology databank to user guidance files of interest to the whole European online user community, e.g., DIANEGUIDE, a database on online databases and databanks available in Europe, and an online directory of information brokers currently active within the EC Member States. Usually these databases are not available elsewhere and some are free of charge. New online information services may request to be hosted by ECHO for an initial experimental period.[35]

(6) Preparatory Activities in Connection with the EC Action Plan for Libraries: IMPACT-1 has allocated 2.5 million ECU for preparatory activities in connection with the Plan which is discussed later on in this article. Within this framework the Commission recently issued two reports useful for libraries that wish to make their automated systems compatible with ISO's Open Systems Interconnection (OSI) model.[36,37] The Commission is also supporting a pilot/demonstration project in which seven national libraries are collaborating to use CD-ROM as a vehicle to improve the interchange of bibliographic records.[34,38] In addition, the Commission is contributing to a pilot/demonstration project aiming at creating an interconnection between three libraries or library networks in France, the UK and the Netherlands, based on OSI standards and aiming at establishing efficient international interlending and messaging services.[34]

In March 1990 an evaluation report of IMPACT-1 was presented to the programme's Senior Officials Advisory Committee (SOAC). This report is based on interviews with and questionnaires sent to senior representatives of the information industry, information policy makers and administrators in Member States. It found a generally supportive response to the activities carried out under IMPACT-1.[39]

An IMPACT-2 programme has been proposed for the period 1991-1995. The budget requested is not exactly known but estimates circulating among insiders range between 50 million and 125 million ECU. The new programme is still being discussed within the Commission secretariat before it goes via the Economic and Social Committee and the European Parliament to the competent Council of Ministers for approval. Until this approval is obtained only very limited activities beyond what is currently going on under IMPACT-1 will be possible (these will have to be financed from so-called minimal budgets as part of the Commission's running budget). The headings of some of the activities of IMPACT-2 have changed name but its objectives and actual contents are very much the same as that of IMPACT-1. There seems to be somewhat more emphasis on the participation of small and medium-sized enterprises in commercial ventures of new information products. The headings read as follows:

Action line 1:	Improving the understanding of the market (in fact this is the continuation of the Information Market Observatory).
Action line 2:	Overcoming legal and administrative barriers.
Action line 3:	Increasing user-friendliness and improving information literacy.
Action line 4:	Supporting strategic information initiatives.

3. SPECIFIC EC ACTIVITIES FOR LIBRARIES

3.1 The "European Library" Idea

This idea is embodied in the Leonardi[40] and Schwencke[41] Resolutions which were presented to the European Parliament in November 1982 and in March 1984 respectively. The Leonardi version of the European Library amounted to the creation of a European depository library which would contain all books published within the EC and which would perform, at Community level, all functions of the national libraries of the Member States. The European Library described in the Schwencke Resolution is still a very ambitious undertaking but is somewhat more realistic. Essentially what is proposed in this Resolution is the creation of a kind of automated central catalogue of references relevant to Europe and covering history and civilization, law and economics, political and social sciences, general cultural and literary studies, documents and studies drawn up by and on behalf of the European Communities, European peace and security policy, developments in Eastern Europe, EC aid to and relations with the "Lomé" developing countries (mostly former colonies of Member States). This central catalogue was to be organized in such a way as to make it possible for users to identify the material which they need and to indicate to them the location where it is available. In addition to the catalogue, enquiry and document delivery services were to be provided as well. The catalogue and associated services facilities were to be located at the European University Institute (EUI) at Florence in Italy. The European Library as such has never been officially established but, in the last few years, the EUI has received about 100,000 ECU each year, under this heading, from EC funds voted by the European Parliament.

There can be no doubt that the above Resolutions have been the starting point for intensified discussion of greater library cooperation in Europe. Their effect on EC library policy and activities is also evident. It is clear that most of the EC activities described in the preceding sections have a bearing on libraries. Nevertheless, the European Communities did not have a library policy as such. Since the Resolutions invited the Commission to take action in the field, it had to do something more explicit. The legal basis for such action was given by a Resolution adopted by the Council of Ministers responsible for cultural affairs on 27 September 1985.[42] This Resolution requests the Commission to define and set up a system, in collaboration with the most important libraries in Europe, that would enable computerized catalogues to be linked up. It also requested the Commission to prepare a possible work programme to speed up the development of library activities "as a major force on the information market in terms of both innovation and innovation support." Resources for at least the initial activities required were to be found within those allocated to the development of the specialized information market in Europe (i.e., the IMPACT programme).

Following this Resolution the Commission formulated its "Action Plan for Libraries."

3.2 The EC Action Plan for Libraries

As a first step the Commission embarked on a number of background studies to assess the overall situation. Among other things these revealed some interesting figures.[43] There are at least 75,000 libraries run by public authorities in the EC. These contain about 1.2 billion books and cost the public sector about 5 billion ECU per year. If libraries of the private sector are added the annual expenditure may be in the order of 10 billion ECU. The library sector employs more than 250,000 people and about 23 per cent of the total EC population are regular library users. The figures quoted reflect the situation in 1985. Of the main medium to large commercial automated library systems known to be installed in Europe (probably about 250 in the EC by 1987), more than 50 per cent stem from non-European suppliers. By comparison, it was estimated that by the end of 1985 there were more than 1,100 commercial turnkey systems installed in North America (excluding library-developed ones) and that the yearly rate of increase is well over 200 in the U.S. European libraries are, therefore, a considerable potential market for appropriate new technology, also and not in the least for potential European suppliers.

Armed with this characteristic economic motivation, in 1987 the Commission prepared a first draft "Plan of Action for Libraries in the EC"[44] and went through an extensive series of meetings and consultations involving a broad spectrum of officials from the library and related sectors, professional organizations and government departments. As a result of second "Draft Plan of Action for Libraries in the EC"[45] was prepared in 1989 which did not differ much from the first except that the budget proposed for the five-year plan was raised from 33 million ECU to 95 million ECU. In spite of extensive preparatory action and meetings in Member States, including the distribution of guidelines and criteria for preparing project proposals,[46] the specific budget allocation for the plan has still not been approved by the Council of Ministers. This is now expected to take place in the course of 1991. The amount proposed for the plan has in any case been considerably reduced (about 26 million ECU for the five years) by the Commission and the Plan is now a component of "a specific programme of research and technological development in the field of Telematic Systems in areas of General Interest (1990-1994)"[47] which is itself part of the "Third Framework Programme on Community Research and Technological Development."

The Plan is an information-technology oriented programme. It relies on a combination of state-of-the-art information technology, the adoption of common standards and intra-European collaboration to secure a firm position for European libraries in the information society and, consequently, to offer users optimum information services as a prerequisite for economic, social and cultural progress.

To achieve these basic objectives, the Plan conceives five so-called action lines within which concrete projects are to be carried out in partnership with the Commission:

1. Library source data projects: setting up computerized national bibliographies where these are lacking, helping to improve existing national computerized bibliographies and union catalogues, support for retrospective conversion of internationally important collections.
2. Projects facilitating the international interconnection of the systems managing these basic data for particular purposes such as shared cataloguing, inter-library loans, etc. As a by-product this should foster the development and application of a range of international standards.
3. Projects to stimulate the provision of innovative library services based on new information technologies and taking into account the different levels of development of library services in Member States.
4. Projects in support of the development of a European market in telematic products and services designed specifically for library services and management requirements. This will include limited initial support for experimental demonstrations of relevant products and services (e.g., software).
5. Projects to stimulate exchange of experience and dissemination of knowledge between those responsible for libraries in Member States and provision of support for the preparation of projects under the other action lines.

The Commission's Action Plan has met with widespread approval in European library circles. In spite of its limited resources, this author believes that the Plan should have a considerable promotional effect on library cooperation in Europe generally and, hopefully, also on the introduction of relevant standards. On the negative side, the Plan has been criticized[48] for giving too much emphasis to national bibliographies, national union catalogues and retrospective conversion (about one third of the proposed budgets) and for not giving more attention to regional discrepancies which are one of the major difficulties impeding Europe-wide interconnection of libraries. Other criticisms which may be mentioned are the relatively low total budget allocation and in particular that of the fifth action line covering the critical areas of continuing education and support for project preparation. As a matter of fact, in the latest proposal before the Council of Ministers,[47] the fifth action line is no longer a separate item but has been subsumed under each of the other action lines. Given the cost involved with the preparation of project proposals and the fact that the Commission will finance only between 10 and 50 per cent of total project costs depending on the circumstances, it is to be feared that only larger and better funded libraries will be able to benefit from the Plan unless additional funds are made available at the national level. This is the case, for example, in the UK where assistance for project formulation is available from the British Library.[49]

3.3 EUROLIB

From what precedes it will be clear that EC information policy, to the extent that it exists as such, is very much oriented towards the introduction of modern information technology and economic considerations (creating an information services market in Europe on a par with those of the US and Japan). The more recent attention for libraries, and in particular the Action Plan for Libraries in the EC, appear almost as an afterthought. So far there has never been a coherent information policy for the internal library and information services of the European Communities either. This has resulted in the creation of incompatible internal library and information systems and duplication of work coupled with less than comprehensive bibliographic control even of EC publications and documentation in the individual institutions.

The first trace of an effort to organize closer cooperation between libraries of the EC institutions is a report on a "Meeting of Librarians-Documentalists of the Institutions of the European Communities, held at Luxembourg on February 19th 1981," which the author found in an internal European Parliament file. It appears from this report that the major concerns were:

- the impending automation of the libraries;
- the need to adopt a common thesaurus;
- "the need . . . to harmonize . . . certain working procedures . . . with a view . . . to avoid duplicating common tasks such as the indexing and cataloguing of Community publications";
- to strengthen formal contacts by means of annual meetings;
- to set up an interinstitutional working group with its secretariat vested in the Commission library.

Between this first meeting and the first EUROLIB[50] meeting on 21 June 1988, organized following an invitation by the Secretary General of the European Parliament, nothing much seems to have happened. In 1988 there was still no common vision of a library policy for the EC institutions. This, notwithstanding the European Parliament Resolutions on the "European Library" and the Commission's Action Plan. The same institutions that produced these grand ideas seemed to ignore completely the specific needs and potential pan-European role of their own libraries. Fortunately, the emergence of EUROLIB has changed this perspective.

EUROLIB Objectives

The basic objective is to establish comprehensive bibliographic control and library and document delivery services in the field of European integration. This is to be achieved by pooling the resources of the library and documentation services in the individual EC institutions within a flexible network of autonomous libraries, combined with strict avoidance of duplication of work and coordination of the various activities of the participants. Part of the general philosophy underlying this basic objective is reliance on state-of-the-art information technology, internal standards and utilization or enhancement of existing resources and infrastructure. As to standards, agreement has been reached on the adoption of ISO's "Open System's Interconnection" concept[24] as the general framework for the envisaged EUROLIB network, on ISO's "Common Command Language"[31] for access to online services and on Unesco's "Common Communication Format"[51] for the exchange of machine-readable bibliographic records.

It is also important to mention that the future EUROLIB network is conceived as an open system. This means that the benefits to be derived from this work-sharing and other forms of cooperation are meant not to be restricted to the staff and users of EC institutions' libraries but to be made available also to other interested libraries and their users, for example European Documentation Centres (EDCs),[52] European Depository Libraries (EPDs),[52] EURO Info Centres[52] and libraries of universities and institutes specializing in European integration. Cooperation should not be confined to the EC area but could eventually be world-wide and include other international organizations such as OECD and the United Nations and its specialized agencies. The anticipated EUROLIB services could be particularly useful for EDCs. DEPs, and EURO Info Centres in Member States, many of which do not have the resources to establish adequate bibliographic control over the EC documentation and publications for which they are the depositories and intended local disseminators of the information content.

The EUROLIB programme is not a duplication of the Action Plan for Libraries in the EC since the latter is specifically aimed at libraries in Member States and not at all at EC institutions' libraries. EUROLIB and the Action Plan, therefore, are two separate initiatives but they are complementary.

The EUROLIB Programme

A detailed outline of the EUROLIB programme is given in an explanatory statement annexed to a Resolution which EUROLIB addressed to the heads of the EC institutions following its third meeting.[53] Brief mention of only some of the core programme elements can be made here.[54]

Fundamental to the entire EUROLIB programme is the establishment of a union catalogue of material on European integration and associated lending and document supply services. This catalogue will contain all original titles present in the individual catalogues. The subject of European integration should thus be covered to a very large extent. Possible gaps should be filled from exchanges with libraries outside the EUROLIB group. Ideally references to periodical articles as well as to monographic material should be included. The necessary measures will have to be taken to enable the delivery of the full text of the material referred to in the catalogue. Closely related to this project is the establishment of a parallel union catalogue of serial titles held by the participating libraries. This should be the basis for an interlending system of periodical articles. As an automatic by-product of the union catalogues, a bibliography on European integration could be published.

Some degree of coordination of acquisitions and conservation as a general backup for subject coverage and document delivery services is envisaged. This coordination will have to take into account the existing archival activities of the European Communities.

Continuing education seminars are also planned. A comprehensive course on EC documentation and exchange of local experiences within this context is the first priority. These seminars will be open to staff of the participating libraries but, resources permitting, to interested outsiders as well.

Current Situation

A feasibility study is under way to determine the technical means and organizational infrastructure necessary to implement the EUROLIB programme. This should include cost estimates for the initial establishment and future development and operation of the programme. The feasibility study will also specify the technical, organizational and financial implications of participation for the libraries of the individual institutions. The study is expected to be ready in the autumn of 1991. The findings will be presented to the administrative heads of the EC institutions with a request for formal approval and funding.

4. OTHER INITIATIVES TOWARDS LIBRARY COOPERATION IN EUROPE

The European Communities are not alone in having taken initiatives towards increased library cooperation in Europe. To complete the picture, the activities of a few other organizations are mentioned below without any claim to comprehensiveness.

4.1 The Council of Europe

The Council of Europe has a wider membership than the European Community. In addition to the twelve EC Member States nine other European states form part of the Council: Austria, Cyprus, Iceland, Liechtenstein, Malta, Norway, Sweden, Switzerland and Turkey. The Council of Europe tends to be a consultative body with as its main task the promotion of greater cooperation in Europe, especially in the fields of parliamentary democracy and human rights. It may be considered as a kind of cultural and geographical counterweight for the largely economically oriented activities of the EC restricted to twelve European states only. With the changing political situation in Eastern Europe and the Soviet Union, the Council is expected to play an increasing role in fostering intensified contact and collaboration throughout Europe.[55]

It is not surprising, therefore, that the Council's role in European library affairs has been of a more "traditional" kind. The Council was instrumental in the establishment of the association of European research libraries (LIBER) (see below) in 1971 which acts as its main adviser in the library field. In the seventies LIBER suggested to the Council activities on a wide range of library matters but lack of interest on the part of the decision making powers in the Council and shortage of funds resulted in very little actually happening. From 1984, however, the Council's interest in library matters was revived. In November 1984 the Council co-sponsored an "advanced research workshop"[56] with the purpose of reviewing the impact of new information technology on library management, resources and cooperation in Europe and North America. One important proposal that emerged from this meeting was the recommendation to set up a European Council on Library Resources similar to the American Council on Library Resources. This gave rise to the establishment of the European Foundation for Library Cooperation (see below) in November 1985.

Following the EC Council of Ministers Resolution on collaboration between libraries in the field of data processing,[42] the Council itself passed a Recommendation[57] on 26 May 1987 on cooperation among research libraries in Europe. This Recommendation urges Member States to take measures to intensify cooperation among libraries in Europe covering every aspect of library activity: cataloguing, creating data bases, facilitating access to data bases and resources, standardization, preservation, work-sharing, etc. The overall aim was stated as making "the enormous data and treasure of European research libraries accessible to as many as possible and as quickly as possible." A suggestion in the Recommendation was to "examine possibilities of promoting or setting up a permanent organizational infrastructure for co-operation among libraries in Europe." This particular idea, no doubt, has inspired the promotors of the European Foundation for Library Cooperation to see their organization as the potential official forum for intra-European library cooperation.

In September 1989 the Council issued another Recommendation[58] on retrospective conversion of library cataloguing to machine-readable forms. This Recommendation reflects the concern of national and large research libraries to computerize their current and historical catalogues. The financial and standardization problems connected with this are well known. The hub of the answer suggested by the Council is selectivity in processing, adoption of ISBDs and UNIMARC as cataloguing standards[59] and additional funding from national and international sources. Typical perhaps for an organization with a strong cultural bias, the Recommendation contains a controversial clause saying that ". . . converted catalogue records should be able to circulate unrestrictedly within and between library networks, without legal or contractual constraints on their use in other members of those networks."

The Council has given a grant to LIBER of about 12,000 US dollars to establish a European register of microform masters. It also promotes a long-term project of storage on optical discs of special collections such as manuscripts and newspapers.[60]

4.2 LIBER *(League des Bibliothèques Européennes de Recherche)*

As mentioned earlier LIBER was founded in 1971 under the auspices of the Council of Europe. Members are national, university and special research libraries from countries that cooperate in the Council for Cultural Cooperation of the Council of Europe. In 1989 there were about 250 members.[61]

LIBER studies a wide range of library related subjects on the occasion of conferences held within the framework of its Annual General Meeting and of seminars of working groups. The results are published in the LIBER Bulletin.

The following current LIBER activities may be mentioned:

- In 1988 LIBER published a directory of library bibliographic networks in Europe.[62] In passing it may be mentioned that of the 35 networks described only three used UNIMARC as their exchange format and none used the CCF[51] for that purpose.
- The LIBER Library Automation Group (LLA) is advising the Council of Europe on retrospective catalogue conversion problems in the form of methodological papers dealing with the aims, format problems, selection criteria for priority processing, and cost of retrospective cataloguing activities.
- LIBER prepared a draft outline for a feasibility study for the establishment of a European Register of Microform Masters. This feasibility study has meanwhile been commissioned by the EC Commission as a preparatory activity to its Action Plan for Libraries in the EC.
- The LIBER Conspectus Group, in collaboration with the Conference of National Librarians in Western Europe, is endeavouring to promote the conspectus method in Europe as an instrument for resource sharing in the fields of collection development, retrospective conversion and conservation and preservation.
- LIBER cooperates with some firms to study library applications of scanning technologies and optimal media.

4.3 EFLC (European Foundation for Library Cooperation)

The European Foundation for Library Cooperation, also known under the name "Groupe de Lausanne," was established on 4 August 1986. Its ambition is to play a role in Europe equivalent to that of the Council on Library Resources in the US. It "aims at strengthening library cooperation in Europe and the management of information resources of libraries for improving user services."[63] To achieve this general aim, EFLC intends to sponsor projects in the areas of resource sharing and access to information (including collection development, interlibrary loans and electronic document delivery), library network development, training and education, preservation and conservation of library materials, and library research. Initially, priority is to be given to the introduction of new technologies and of education and training.[64]

EFLC seems to be mainly interested in stimulating cooperation between research libraries, defined as being university and national libraries in the first instance, but it seems to be open in principle to a wider group, including public libraries.[65] As a matter of fact, one of the Board Members advocates a leading role for EFLC in the gradual establishment of a kind of "European Library" composed mainly of a distributed network of European national libraries.[66] Two other Board members seem to consider that EFLC—without, however, naming it explicitly in the sources upon which this remark is based[48,67]—should become the official international body to represent library interests in Europe and in particular that it should function as a European professional organization to represent the interests of the profession at intergovernmental level, e.g., at the level of the EC and the Council of Europe.

In reality, EFLC has so far not been given any formal representative mandate nor substantial funds to enable it to finance library projects. It is sponsoring a project of computerization, including retroconversion and networking, of eleven archeological libraries in Athens but, at the time of writing, a feasibility and development study had been prepared but no funding had been obtained. At the First European Conference on Library Automation and Networking which EFLC organized in Brussels on 9-11 May 1990, the idea of becoming a formal representative organization for the European library profession was aired from the Chair but did not meet with any clear-cut positive response from the audience.[68]

4.4 OCLC

It appears to this author that a discussion of library cooperation in Europe is not complete without at least mentioning the "Online Computer Library Center" incorporated at Dublin, Ohio, USA. This is because of the sheer size of its operations and its active presence on the European market since 1981[69,70]. Indeed, towards the end of 1988, the OCLC online union catalogue was reported to contain 18 million records of which about 4.5 million were Library of Congress records. In addition to the supply of bibliographic records on various media, OCLC offers a variety of other services such as shared cataloguing, retrospective conversion, acquisition of any type of library material and interlibrary lending facilities. In late 1988, it counted 5,500 actively participating libraries and served directly or indirectly more than 9,500 institutions in more than 25 countries, of which 79 in Europe.[62] Whereas sample studies have indicated that OCLC coverage of bibliographic records is often as high as 90 per cent or more of local database holdings in the US, equivalent figures for Europe are much less, often well under 50 per cent. It is to be expected, however, that, as more European customers join the network, coverage of European material will improve.

So far there is no library network in Europe that comes anywhere near the data base size of OCLC. The largest database reported in the LIBER Directory[62] is that of PICA (Dutch Centre for Library Automation) with 4.5 million records. Some of these European networks, including PICA, are customers of OCLC. It can therefore be said that by far the largest operator on the European library networking scene is a US concern, albeit a not-for-profit one. At the same time there is plenty of scope left for competition. OCLC is known for its relatively low-quality cataloguing. It has only recently begun to provide subject access through its Epic and FIRST-SEARCH end-user services, although this is indirectly available from two other US firms: BRS and Blackwell North America. OCLC is in any case working on an extensive modernization programme, called the Oxford Project, which will enhance retrieval and allow subject access by subject headings and classification number. It should be interesting eventually to examine the extent to which OCLC may have had an impact on library networking in Europe and to compare it with the expected impact of the EC Action Plan for Libraries.

5. CONCLUDING REMARKS

The first question which comes to mind is whether Europe and in particular the EC will succeed in its objective of catching up with Japan and the US in order to secure for itself a place on a par with these two countries in the post-industrial information society. This is a very difficult question to answer. What can be said with certainty, however, is that a considerable additional effort will have to be made. Only when investment levels in research and development reach those of the two main competitors will there be a realistic prospect for achieving the aim. It is clear that the main effort will have to come from the private sector. The stimulating efforts undertaken by national governments and those by the EC outlined in this article are certainly a move in the right direction and have resulted in greater awareness of the problem and increased efforts towards intra-European cooperation. The least one can say is that the battle has not yet been definitely lost. Of capital importance in all this is the creation of a genuinely barrier-free European market. Undoubtedly continuing progress has been made ever since the establishment of the European Economic Community but the highly publicized completion of the single European market by the end of 1992 may not yet be as complete as it should be. Indeed it is unlikely that the indirect barriers to the free flow of goods and services will all be effectively removed. Persistent different national legislations and tax systems, for example, will take more time to be completely harmonized. The complete neutralization of the national telecommunications monopolies, to mention only this sector which is so important from the point of view of an integrated European information services market, is a case in point.

The next question is, what is the particular situation within this broader economic context of European library and information services, in other words, of the European information industry? The answer is that the general considerations just mentioned apply fully also to the library and information sector. It is worth adding, however, that language barriers and those inherent with the as yet imperfect single European market are especially difficult obstacles in competing with the US and Japan because of their hindering effect on the creation of economies of scale. The various EC initiatives for stimulating the EC information industry market are likely to have their main impact at the psychological and promotional level. Eventually they may prove to have their principal effect on the public sector, e.g., on libraries and government information services. The private information industry sector goes where the profit is and needs little help in doing that. It expects only the removal of trade-barriers such as different national legislations, regulations and state monopolies. The sooner all these can be removed, the sooner competition on an equal basis with the US and Japan can take place and, just as important, the sooner Europe will be able to take advantage of the necessary economies of scale.

The author wishes to make two final remarks particularly concerning libraries.

The first is that EC library policy and in particular the EC Action Plan for Libraries will need to concentrate on the stimulation of sectoral library networks rather than on networks of national libraries and the conversion of their current and historical catalogues, at least in terms of relative shares in dedicated resources. Without denying the general importance of national libraries and the information they have to offer, increased efforts to set up sectoral library networks and services is likely to be more immediately beneficial, especially in the present climate of limited and even shrinking resources devoted to libraries. Successful international cooperative networks such as AGRIS,[71] DOCPAL,[72] the EAHIL[73] interlibrary lending network, and INIS[74] prove the point. In the near future EUROLIB may provide an additional example of a successful sectoral library network.

The last remark concerns the temptation for some libraries and their information services to try and hope unreservedly on the nowadays popular commercial bandwagon. If the profit motive is to be applied to all information services indiscriminately, this will result in most of them becoming out of reach of the majority of potential users, to become the exclusive preserve of the financially more powerful (groups rather than individuals). By way of illustration it is interesting to mention the reported protest by graduate students of London University against proposals to charge them for using the library.[75]

In the opinion of the author, libraries should seek to maintain their traditional cultural role of disseminating information to their patrons free or at affordable rates even if this implies a certain amount of public funding. This, of course, does not mean that they should not endeavour to make use of advanced information technology and strive for greater efficiency and cost consciousness. However, the advantages to be derived from better information management of this kind should be passed on to their users in terms of better services at low cost rather than satisfy ambitions of total cost recovery or maximization of profit. This applies in particular to library and information services in the public sector that have their fixed and basic operating costs paid from tax payers' money.

There should be no embarrassment in catering also, if not necessarily exclusively, for the "lower end of the market," for the "information have nots." The "information haves" and in particular those that use financial information services are very capable of looking after themselves. From the point of view of general cultural, educational and social preoccupation the hole in the market is the provision of adequate and economic information services to the general public, i.e., in the first place to individuals who cannot afford to pay full commercial rates for all their perceived and potential information needs. Catering for this category of users should be one of the objectives beyond the quest for adopting up-to-date information technology, resource-sharing, networking, etc. Such a more traditional and humanistic outlook for libraries should be one of their specific contributions to giving a better social balance to the emerging information society in general and in particular to EC policy in this field which tends to see everything too much through the economic looking glass.

REFERENCES

The following periodical or name abbreviations are used:

CEC = Commission of the European Communities
OOPEC = Office for Official Publications of the European Communities
OJ = Official Journal of the European Communities
ISO = International Organization for Standardization

1. MALLEY, Ian. National and international imperatives of a UK national information policy. *Aslib Proceedings 42(3)*, March 1990, p. 92.
2. Ibid., p. 89.
3. Ibid., p. 94.
4. CUNNINGHAM, George. EUROLIS. A Report on Library and Information Services Activity in the European Community and the Council of Europe. London, the Library Association, November 1988, pp. 90-91.
5. JANSEN VAN ROSENDAAL, C. European information policy situation. *Aslib Proceedings 36(1)*, January 1984, pp. 15-23. 6. IRWIN, F.B. Electronic Publishing for Business and Finance: Present Situation and Future Developments. *In*: MASTRODDI, F. (ed.). Electronic Publishing: The New Way to Communicate. Proceedings of the Symposium held in Luxembourg, 5-7 November 1986. Brussels-Luxembourg, CEC, 1987, (EUR. 10978 EN), pp. 161-168.
7. UNGERER, Herbert and COSTELLO, Nicholas. Telecommunications in Europe. Free choice for the user in Europe's 1992 market. The challenge for the European Community. Luxembourg, OOPEC, 1988, pp. 94-95.
8. GREWLICH, K.W. and PEDERSEN, F.H. (eds). Power and Participation in an information society. Luxembourg, CEC, 1984, 298 p. (Based on a Conference which took place on 9-12 November 1981 in Copenhagen within the framework of the FAST-Forecasting and Assessment in the field of Science and Technology—programme.)
9. Ibid., pp. v-vii and 5-10.
10. KALAYDJIAN, B. Notice 19—La recherche et la technologie. *In*: L'Europe des Communautés. Paris, La Documentation française, 1989, 8 p.
11. ECU = European Currency Unit, an accounting unit which is determined on the basis of a "basket" of specific amounts of the national currencies of the EC Member States. At the time of writing (December 1990), the official ECU rate was: 1 ECU = 1.3789 US dollars.
12. CADIOU, Jean-Marie. Le programme Esprit. *Annales des Mines*. Numéro spécial, February 1989, pp. 60-64.
13. L'avenir de la politique de la Communauté Economique Européenne en matière de science et de technologie. *Journal officiel de la République Française 1988(3)*, Friday, 19 February 1988, pp. 65-67.
14. HOBDAY, Mike. The European Semiconductor Industry: Resurgence and

Rationalisation. *Journal of Common Market Studies 28(2)*, December 1989, pp. 155-186.

15. KRIEGER MYTELKA, Lynn and DELAPIERRE, Michel. The Alliance Strategies of European Firms in the Information Technology Industry and the Role of ESPRIT. *Journal of Common Market Studies 26(2)*, December 1987, pp. 231-253.

16. UNGERER, Herbert and COSTELLO, Nicholas. Op. cit., pp. 153-157, 173-176.

17. Council Recommendation of 22 December 1986 on the coordinated introduction of the Integrated Services Digital Network (ISDN) in the European Community (86/659/EEC), *OJ*, L 382, 31.12.1986, p. 36.

18. Council Resolution of 18th July 1989 on the strengthening of the coordination for the introduction of the Integrated Services Digital network (ISDN) in the European Community up to 1992 (89/C 196/04). *OJ*, C 196, 1.8.1989, pp. 4-6.

19. CEC. Progress Report 1989 concerning the co-ordinated introduction of the Integrated Services Digital Network (ISDN) in the European Community (COM(90)123 Final). Brussels, 23 March 1990, 28 p.

20. UNGERER, Herbert and COSTELLO, Nicholas. Op. cit., pp. 51-55.

21. Council Decision of 13 December 1982 relating to the coordination of the activities of the Member States and community institutions with a view to assessing the need for, and preparing proposals for setting up, a Community interinstitutional information system (82/869/EEC). *OJ*, L 368/40, 28 December 1982, pp. 40-41.

22. Undated internal CEC document describing the tasks to be performed by the contractor to carry out the "INSIS Strategic Study," a provisional version of which was completed in December 1990.

23. Project SAINT-1. Task 1. Simplification of Access to Information Using Normalized Transfer. State-of-the-art Analysis. October, 26th. 1988 (SAINT 87-03-19).

24. ISO 7498. Information Processing Systems—Open Systems Interconnection—Basic Reference Model. Geneva, ISO, 1979.

25. Council Decision 84/567/EEC on a Community programme for the development of a specialized information market in Europe. *OJ*, L 314/19 of 4 December 1984, p. 19 ff.

26. Council Decision of 26 July 1988 covering the establishment of a plan of action for setting up an information services market (88/524/EEC). *OJ*, L 288/39 of 21 October 1988, p. 39 ff.

27. UNGERER, Herbert and COSTELLO, Nicholas. Op. cit., pp. 113-116.

28. *I'M—Information Market No. 64*, September-October 1990, p. 1.

29. "Barriers to the free flow of books," published by ELP (the working group of European Librarians and Publishers) and quoted in *I'M—Information Market No. 65*, November 1990-January 1991, p. 9.

30. MARTYN, John. EEC Information Market and Library Programmes. *Library and Information Briefings*. London, British Library Research and Develop-

ment Department and Library and Information Technology Centre, Polytechnic of Central London, September 1989, 11 p.

31. ISO 8777. Documentation—Commands for Interactive Text Searching. Geneva, ISO, 1990.

32. *I'M—Information Market No. 61*, March-April 1990, p. 3.

33. CEC. Guidelines for improving the synergy between the public and private sectors in the information market. Luxembourg, OOPEC, 1989, 13 p.

34. *I'M*. Op. cit., No 61, pp. 1-3 and 11.

35. For more details on ECHO a brochure is available from the ECHO Customer Service, P.O.B. 2373, L-1023 Luxembourg: "ECHO Databases and Services." ECHO users receive a newsletter "ECHO News."

36. CAILLOUX, J.M. (ed). Proceedings of the workshop dedicated to the use of OSI for libraries. Luxembourg, OOPEC, 1989, 140 p. (EUR 12436 EN/FR).

37. CAILLOUX, J.M.; CASIMIR, C. OSI model for library applications. A tutorial. Luxembourg, OOPEC, 1989, 143 p. (EUR 12437 EN).

38. BUCKLEY, Barbara J. The European Cooperative CD-ROM Project. *In*: DEMPSEY, Lorcan. Bibliographic Access in Europe: First International Conference. The proceedings of a conference organized by the Centre for Bibliographic Management and held at the University of Bath, 14-17 September 1989. Aldershot, Hants. Gower, 1990, pp. 190-197.

39. *I'M*. Op. cit., No. 63, July-August 1990, pp. 1-3.

40. Motion for a Resolution (Document 1-794/82) tabled by M. Leonardi et al. at the Sitting of the European Parliament of 15 November 1982.

41. Report drawn up on behalf of the Committee on Youth, Culture, Education, Information and Sport, on the creation of a European Library. Part A: Motion for a Resolution. Part B: Explanatory Statement (Documents 1-1524/83/A of 15 March 1984 and 1-1524/83/B of 26 March 1984). This Resolution was adopted by the European Parliament on 30 March 1984 (see *OJ*, C 117 of 30 April 1984).

42. Council Resolution. Council and the ministers with responsibility for cultural affairs, meeting within the Council of 27 September 1985 on collaboration between libraries in the field of data processing (85/C 271/01). *OJ.*, C 271/1, 23 October 1985.

43. Taken from: RAMSDALE, Ph. A study of library economics in the European Communities. Luxembourg, OOPEC, 1988, 158 p. (EUR 11546 EN) and quoted in: Communication from the Commission and Draft Resolution on the bringing into effect of a plan of action at Community level aimed at library cooperation based on the application of new information technologies, Brussels, 16 May 1989, 13 p. (COM(89) 234 final).

44. Plan of Action for Libraries in the EC—First Draft for Discussion. Revision 2. Luxembourg, 8 October 1987, 22 p. (internal document prepared by Directorate General XIII of the Commission).

45. An Assessment of Comments received on the First Draft for Discussion of a Plan of Action for Libraries in the E.C. Annex II: Second Draft Plan of Action

for Libraries in the E.C. Luxembourg, 28 February 1989, 22 p. (internal document prepared by Directorate General XIII of the Commission).

46. CEC. DG XIII-B. Action Plan for Libraries: Guidelines and Criteria for Projects. February, 1990.

47. CEC. Proposal for a *Council Decision* concerning a specific programme of research and technological development in the field of Telematic Systems in areas of General Interest (1990-1994) (presented by the Commission). Brussels, 23 May 1990 (COM(90) 155 final-SYN 260), 25 p.

48. See e.g., WALCKIERS, Marc. European Health Librarians Facing 1992. *LIBER Bulletin 35*. General Assembly Madrid 1989. Bremen, 1990, pp. 74-78.

49. MARTYN, John. *Op. cit.*, p. 10.

50. The full name of EUROLIB is: "European Community and Associated Institutions Library Cooperative Group." At the time of writing EUROLIB membership comprised the libraries of the following institutions:

- the Commission of the European Communities
- the Office of Official Publications of the European Communities
- the Council of Ministers
- the Court of Justice
- the Court of Auditors
- the Economic and Social Committee
- the European Parliament
- the European Investment Bank
- the European Institute of Public Administration
- the European University Institute
- the Council of Europe
- the College of Europe.

Expected to join soon are the libraries of

- the European Foundation for the Improvement of Living and Working Conditions;
- the European Centre for the Development of Vocational Training (CEDEFOP).

51. SIMMONS, P.; HOPKINSON, A. (eds). CCF: The Common Communication Format. Second edition. Paris, Unesco, 1988 (PGI-88/WS/2).

52. European Documentation Centres and European Depository Libraries are given extensive EC documentation collections by the Commission for the purpose of facilitating research and study related to EC affairs in Member States. Smaller collections of basic EC documentation are kept in European Reference Centres (ERCs). More recently EURO Info Centres, also referred to as "Euro guichets," have been established in Member States for the particular benefit of small and medium-sized enterprises to enable these to have rapid access to EC information of interest to them. For a critical article discussing EDCs within the context of EC

information policy, see HARBORD, Peter. European Documentation Centres and the Commission's Information Policy: a view over the shoulder. *European Access 1989(1)*, February, pp. 27-28.

53. RESOLUTION adopted by the European Community and Associated Institutions Library Cooperative Group (EUROLIB) and presented on its behalf by its Chairman to the Administrative heads of the participating institutions. Part A: Resolution (EUROLIB/RES-A/28.04.89). Part B: Explanatory Statement (EUROLIB/RES-B/18.08.89).

54. For a more detailed account, see DIERICKX, Harold. EUROLIB. *European Access*, December 1990, pp. 28-29.

55. CUNNINGHAM, George. Op. cit., pp. 11-13 and 76-85.

56. LIEBAERS, H. et al. (eds). New Information Technologies and Libraries. Dordrecht, D. Reidel Publishing Company, 1985, 364 p.

57. [COUNCIL OF EUROPE]. Recommendation No. R(87)11 of the Committee of Ministers to Member States on Co-operation among Research Libraries in Europe (adopted by the Committee of Ministers on 26 May 1987 . . .).

58. [COUNCIL OF EUROPE]. Recommendation No. R(89) 11 of the Committee of Ministers to Member States on retrospective conversion of library catalogues to machine-readable forms (adopted by the Committee of Ministers on 19 September 1989 . . .).

59. RAU, Peter. Reconversion in Europe: the Council of Europe's initiatives. *In*: DEMPSEY, Lorcan. Op. cit., pp. 161-169.

60. KOCH, Hans-Albrecht. Library cooperation within the Ligue des Bibliothèques Européennes de Recherche (LIBER). *In*: HELAL, Ahmed and WEISS, Joachim W. International Library Cooperation. Essen, Essen University Library, 1988, pp. 52-68.

61. KOCH, Hans-Albrecht, LIBER and the Library Action Plan of the European Communities. *LIBER Bulletin 35*. General Assembly Madrid 1989. Bremen, 1990 pp. 72-73.

62. Library Bibliographic Networks in Europe. A LIBER directory. The Hague, Nederlands Bibliotheek en Lektuur Centrum (NBLC), 1988, 83 p.

63. See pamphlet (undated): "EFLC-European Foundation for Library Cooperation (Groupe de Lausanne)." Available from the EFLC Secretariat, B.P. 237, B-1040 Brussels, Belgium.

64. GOOSSENS, Paula. Proposals for Library Cooperation in Europe. *In*: LIEBAERS, H. et al. Op. cit., pp. 137-148.

65. LIEBAERS, H. Towards a European Council of Research Libraries. *In*: LIEBAERS, H. et al. Op. cit., pp. 37-42.

66. GOOSSENS, Paula. The European Library: A summing up. *In*: DEMPSEY, Lorcan. Op. cit., pp. 289-303.

67. CUNNINGHAM, George. Op. cit., pp. 38, 83, 93.

68. Personal recollection of the author who attended.

69. SAFFADY, W. OCLC. *Library Technology Reports 24(6)*, November-December 1988, p. 744 ff.

70. BUCKLE, David. European and North American Library Co-operation —

Co-operation Opportunities for Resource Sharing. *In*: HELAL, Ahmed and WEISS, Joachim W. Op. cit., pp. 205-219.
  71. International Information System for the Agricultural Sciences and Technology.
  72. Latin American Population Documentation System.
  73. European Association for Health Information and Libraries.
  74. International Nuclear Information System.
  75. *Cablis* No. 19, July 1990, p. 2.

ANNEX

ACCESS TO EC INFORMATION – A FEW HINTS

To deal comprehensively with sources of EC information and related tools of bibliographic control is impossible within the scope of an article. Having nevertheless been encouraged by the editor to try and do "something" in that direction, some of the major tools of bibliographic control are outlined in this annex. This is by no means a complete exposition and sources or works that are not mentioned are, therefore, not necessarily of secondary importance. The expert reader may find little if anything new here. On the other hand, it is hoped that the less well informed reader may be put on the right track to becoming more familiar with the intricate subject of EC information.

1. General Descriptive Sources

Only a very few are mentioned but they are comprehensive guides to EC documentation including, in some cases, a description of the legal and administrative framework within which the European Community operates.

1.1 THOMSON, Ian. *The Documentation of the European Communities: A Guide*. London, Mansell Publishing Limited, 1989, 396 p. ISBN 0-7201-2022-5.

The stated aim of this book is "to describe the current range of publicly available printed documentation produced by the EC" (p. viii). It reflects the situation as it was in early 1988 (p. ix). There is no doubt that the author achieves his objective admirably well.

In ten introductory pages the history of the European Communities is sketched, its main institutions are mentioned and the production and distribution process of EC documentation is outlined. The bulk of the book is taken up by a detailed discussion of the documentation produced by the individual institutions. One of the interesting features is that the various titles are described within a broader description of the objectives and administrative structure of the producing organizations. Treatment of the legal documentation, for example, is not just a listing of series titles and their coverage but includes an explanation of the EC legal system and the respective roles played by the individual institutions within that legislative and regulatory framework.

In addition to printed documentation, the book lists the EC online databases with a line or two on content, useful contact addresses and sources for further information.

There is also a wealth of addresses: the location worldwide of EC information Offices, External Delegations, Sales Offices, European Documentation Centres, Depository Libraries et al.

A detailed index completes the work. Little if anything seems to have escaped the attention of the author. To keep track of the ongoing evolution on the EC publication scene, there is another essential source:

1.2 *Directory of EC Information Sources*, published annually, in English and French, by EURO CONFIDENTIAL, avenue Paola, 43, B-1330 Rixensart-Belgium. No ISSN or ISBN; price of the 1990 volume: 7,700 Belgian francs, ca. 260 US dollars.

This massive directory (the 1990 edition counts 731 A-4 size pages) gives much the same information as the previous source but has the advantage that it is updated every year. For every title it gives: contents/subject matter, authorship, frequency, language(s) of text, price and full address for ordering. Many of these entries cover a full page.

In addition to the detailed description of the publications, there is an indication of the 'information structure,' i.e., documentary production and distribution channels of the various EC institutions. In the case of the Commission there is also an exposition of the administrative structure and the main services, their fields of competence and names and addresses of officials who may be contacted for particular types of information. This type of more general information on the Commission covers about 65 pages of the 1990 Directory. The information on titles, databases and addresses of European Documentation Centres in different parts of the world takes about 130 pages. The description of the commission's statistical publications fills a separate section of 26 pages.

Other interesting features of the Directory are:

- A list of press agencies, news agencies and other independent information bodies providing regular information on the European Community. The list includes detailed contents description of the various sources and subscription prices.
- Consultants specializing in EC matters.
- Lawyers and legal advisers specializing in EC matters.

1.3   HANSON, Terry. *A survey of European Communities databases*. Aslib Proceedings 42(6), June 1990, pp. 171-188.

This is a comprehensive survey of 'publicly available databases produced by the European Community, the databases produced from EC information by private companies and the principal database services of private companies whose coverage of EC affairs is particularly good.' A brief description of contents is provided as well as contact addresses and cost.

There are simply too many EC databases to mention them in this article. Full information is given in the Hanson article. For any reader who may not be familiar with EC databases at all, it is worth noting that the EC's comprehensive legal database is CELEX, available on the Commission's own commercial host "Eurobases" (Commission of the European Communities, 200 rue de la Loi, B-1049 Brussels) and on a number of other commercial hosts, including Profile Information Services (Sunbury House, PO Box 12, Sunbury on Thames, Middlesex TW16 7UD, UK). The latter has only a limited version of CELEX. To keep abreast of current EC issues and in particular of the run-up to the completion of the internal market and related questions in 1993, SCAD may be consulted (host: Eurobases). Also available on Eurobases is ECLAS, the online catalogue of the Central Library of the Commission.

The same author has produced a *Directory of European Community and Related Databases*, published by the European Information Association (EIA) in 1991, 78 p., ISBN 0-948272-24-4. Available from the EIA, Publications Officer: EDC, George Edwards Library, University of Surrey, Guildford GU2 5XH, UK. The contents is similar to that of the article in Aslib Proceedings but the presentation is in a standardized tabular form. In addition to database descriptions there are indexes by database category (bibliographic, factual, legal, statistical) and by host or distributor, as well as a bibliography.

Regular updates on EC databases are provided in *European Access* (see below).

1.4 *European Access—The Current Awareness Bulletin to the Policies and Activities of the European Communities*. Published by Chadwyck-Healey in association with the UK Offices of the European Commission. ISSN: 0264-7362. The 1990 subscription price for six issues was 160 dollars.

The editor is Ian Thomson who contributes regular bibliographic reviews on all aspects of EC policy and activities and on particular topics (e.g., internal market developments, European political union). Terry Hanson writes a regular 'EC Databases column.' Each issue contains a 'Chronology of events in the European Community.' In summary, one can say that the journal provides an ongoing chronicle as well as a wealth of bibliographic information on EC events, policies and programmes. As such it constitutes, together with the works mentioned above, an effective tool for bibliographic control of EC developments and documentation and a means of keeping up-to-date.

2. Publications to Keep Up-to-Date:

In addition to *European Access*, the following are good sources for remaining in touch with ongoing EC affairs:

2.1 The Financial Times (London)

All aspects of EC policy and events are covered with the typical F.T. breadth and depth.

2.2 Agence Europe's Europe Daily Bulletin. No. ISSN.

This 18-page bulletin is published five times a week and has a monthly index which is cumulated at the end of each year. The 1990 subscription rate was 40,000 B.F. (approximately 1,330 US dollars) and includes a number of supplements. The Bulletin is published in English, French, Italian and Spanish. It is available from the Luxembourg Office: 32, rue Philippe II, BP 428, L-2014 Luxembourg. Perhaps the most comprehensive independent news service on EC affairs.

2.3 The weekly AGRA EUROPE, ISSN 0002-1024.

Available from 25, Frant Road, Tunbridge Wells, Kent TN2 5JT, UK. The 1991 subscription price is 715 UK pounds (ca. 1,430 US dollars).
In addition to the weekly, several other publications on agriculture and fisheries are produced by AGRA EUROPE. Some online services are also offered.

2.4 I'M – Information Market (ISSN 0256-5066).

Published by Directorate General XIII of the Commission of the European Communities, available free of charge from: Information Market, P.O. Box 2373, L-1023 Luxembourg. It gives short news items on the information market and industry, mainly, but not exclusively, in Europe, and on related EC activities and programmes.

2.5 ECHO News.

A bi-monthly bulletin available free of charge to users of databases distributed by the EC host 'ECHO.' Available from the same address as that for I'M.

3. Catalogues of the Office for Official Publications of the European Communities (OOPEC)

3.1 Publications of the European Communities

A catalogue listing all monograph, series and periodical titles is issued quarterly by OOPEC under the above title. The fourth issue each year is cumulative for the entire year. It can be obtained free of charge from OOPEC in Luxembourg or from the sales offices printed on the catalogue. It is available separately in all nine Community languages including English.
A classified section lists titles of monographs, series and periodicals under 22 headings, themselves further subdivided. There are also two separate alphabetical lists of periodical and series titles as well as an alphabetical index of titles of monographs and series.
It should be noted that many free items and EC reports or documents published by commercial publishers are not listed in this catalogue.

3.2 Documents

This is a monthly catalogue which is cumulated yearly. It lists references to the following publicly available titles which are generally known as "documents":

1. COM Documents published by the Commission. These are not listed in the publications catalogue described in Section 3.1 above.
2. European Parliament Reports prepared by different Parliamentary Committees and which obtain a "DOC number" after they have been adopted in plenary session.
3. The Opinions and Reports of the Economic and Social Committee of the EC.

The documents catalogue has a classified index similar to that of the publications catalogue, an alphabetical index of entries taken from the EUROVOC Thesaurus, and a numerical index listing documents numbers is ascending order and the corresponding microfiche numbers.

The catalogue can be obtained in all nine EC languages, free of charge, from the OOPEC in Luxembourg or from local sales offices.

3.3 The European Community as a Publisher

This catalogue is aimed at the general public and is an extract of the publications catalogue (cf., Section 3.1) but it often contains titles which are not listed there. It appears annually.

It is available free of charge from the OOPEC or sales offices, in the nine EC official languages.

3.4 EUROSTAT Catalogue

Contains references to the Commission's statistical publications, classified by subject and indicating the medium of publication (paper, magnetic tape or disc, online).

This is an annual catalogue, published in English, French and German. It is also free of charge and available from OOPEC or local sales offices.

4. Official Journal of the European Communities

This is published daily in nine separate editions, one for each official Community language, including English.

It consists of five separately issued parts:

1. 'L' series: Legislation.
   Regulations, Directives and Decisions by the Council of Ministers and the Commission.
2. 'C' series: Information and Notices
   All kinds of information and communications emanating from the different EC institutions, e.g., job vacancy announcements, Resolutions by the Council of Ministers and by the European Parliament, minutes of the plenary sessions of the European Parliament, Opinions of the Economic and Social Committee, summary information on judgements and other activities by the Court of Justice.
3. 'S' series: Supplement
   Tenders for works and supply contracts issued by public authorities in Member States.
4. Annex: Debates of the European Parliament
   The full text of the debates and oral questions submitted during the plenary sessions of the Parliament are reproduced in the Annex.
5. Index: The Index to the Official Journal is published monthly and is cumulated annually. There is a 'methodological' part listing legislation in numerical order and an alphabetical part with terms taken from the EUROVOC multilingual thesaurus, jointly developed by and for the purposes of the OOPEC and the European Parliament. On the whole the index leaves something to be desired and covers effectively only the 'L' series and the part in the 'C' series relating to the Court of Justice. A very useful description of the Official Journal is given in the above mentioned book by Thomson.

5. Tools of Bibliographic Control

One way or another the publications mentioned in the preceding sections, especially those in section 3 and the Index to the Official Journal, are all tools of bibliographic control. Some additional bibliographic aids are:

- List of pending (Commission) Proposals: irregular (once or twice a year); issued as a COM Document.
- Commission proposals on which the European Parliament has delivered an opinion, now pending before the Council. Issued irregularly as a COM Document.
- SCAD Bulletin.
- SCAD online database (see above — same content as SCAD Bulletin).
- CELEX online database (see above).
- Directory of Community Legislation in Force and other acts of the Community institutions. The Directory is updated every six months.
- European Communities legislation: current status. Butterworths, 1988- .
- Encyclopaedia of European Community law. Sweet and Maxwell, 1974- .
- Guide to EC Legislation. North-Holland, 1982- .
- Guide to EC Court Decisions. North-Holland, 1982- .
- Commission of the European Communities. Recent publications on the European Communities received by the Library. ISSN 0257-1080.
 This is a monthly catalogue, the December issue is cumulative for the current year. It lists all items catalogued by the Central Library of the Commission. As from 1989 EC publications and documents are not included because they are listed in the OOPEC catalogues. In addition to full bibliographic descriptions there are author, title, keyword (taken from the Macrothesaurus) and geographical indexes.

All these access tools are very useful but not a single one of them covers *all* EC publications and documents and it is not even sure whether together they are fully comprehensive. No doubt many users would like to have an integrated, timely, comprehensive and easy facility to access EC information. To create such a tool is one of the objectives of EUROLIB (see above).

6. 'First Aid'

In many countries there are EC information offices or other sources of EC information which may be contacted directly. If they do not have the information they should be in a position to indicate where it can be obtained.

European Documentation Centres (EDCs) are located within university or similar institutions which have teaching and/or research programmes in the field of European integration. They receive the complete range of EC publications. Some of them receive a selection only, adapted to their specific fields of interest.

Depository Libraries (DEPs) make the same documentation available to the public at large. Normally they are national libraries, in some countries university libraries. Some have the full range, others only basic documentation on the European Communities.

European Reference Centres (ERCs) are also primarily based in academic institutions. They receive some basic EC documentation and reference lists of EC publications.

More recently *EURO Info Centres* have been created in Member States with the aim of providing information on EC matters to the small- and medium-sized business sector. They are also referred to as European Business Information Centres or EURO-guichets. They have a relevant selection of EC documentation and have access to EC online databases.

The full list of addresses of EDCs, DEPs and ERCs, including those in Canada and the USA, can be obtained from: Commission of the European Communities, DG X-Information, Communication and Culture, University Information, 200 rue de la Loi, B-1049 Brussels, Belgium.

For the USA and Canada the following useful addresses may be noted:

USA

European Community Information Office (*):

(a) 2100 M. Street, N.W.
Suite 707
Washington, D.C. 20037
Tel. (202)862-9500
*Also sales office

(b) 1 Dag Hammarskjöld Plaza
245 East 47th Street
New York, N.Y. 10017
Tel. (212)371-3804

(c) 44 Montgomery Street
Suite 2715
San Francisco, CA 94104

Canada

European Community Information Office:

    Office Tower
    Suite 1110
    350 Sparks Street
    Ottawa, Ontario KIR 7S8
    Tel. 2386464

OOPEC Sales Office:

    Renouf Publishing Co. Ltd.
    61 Sparks Street
    Ottawa, Ontario K1P 5R1
    Tel. Toll Free 1 (800) 2674164

Cooperation Among Libraries in Europe: Current Realities, Future Prospects

Paula Goossens

Cooperation is the key of the future progress of the library community in Europe. Although interinstitutional library collaboration has proven to be very difficult in the past, it must become a reality in the future. As we approach 1992, the need of effective and efficient cooperation intensifies. Fortunately, the technical possibilities for realizing this goal also become more and more available.

Cooperation on different levels has long been recognized as an ideal, but the realization of this goal has been slow to materialize. In the past, major efforts for collaboration were limited to libraries collection building and conservation. Also library automation started with local activities concentrating exclusively on purely clerical functions. Services to the users have been neglected for a long time. Fortunately, the situation is now changing. Progressively, institutions have refocused interests on making their collections more accessible. User friendly OPAC's, worldwide available, and ILL developments become an important issue. The needs of users finally have begun to be taken into consideration. This is timely because our information based society offers new opportunities, and we have to seize them and come into the front-line of progress, giving our patrons all the information they so badly need.

In fact, the unprecedented volume of publications, the severe economic constraints, and the growing expectations of users are forcing libraries in Europe to work more and more together. Given the

---

Paula Goossens is with the European Library Automation Group and Koninklijke Bibliotheek Albert I, Brussels, Belgium.

breadth and depth of users' demands, no single institution can remain self-sufficient if they are to truly provide broad-based services. Access strategies must be developed whereby the resources of individual collections can be shared across geopolitical boundaries.

REQUIREMENTS FOR COOPERATION

A willingness to cooperation is essential for success. With such an attitude, an adequate infrastructure can be built with purposeful leadership, managerial skills, adequate funding, and appropriate tools. The European Community launched a plan of action for libraries in the EC,[1] with partial funding for international cooperative projects. The new working tools created by technological innovation have served to stimulate a favourable and feasible climate for cooperation. Automation and networking capabilities have opened the door to more and better collaboration within the library community. In this article we will mainly concentrate on the technical requirements for cooperation. Standardization is the key to further progress in this field. We have only to look to the United States for an example of the utility of interinstitutional cooperation and standardization. First of all, the AACRII (the second edition of the Anglo-American Cataloguing Rules) has become the norm for the bibliographic description of collections in most organizations. For the intellectual description of the publications, the subject indexing, the LCSH (Library of Congress Subject Headings), the LC (Library of Congress) Classification and the DDC (Dewey Decimal Classification) have emerged as standards.

Effective cooperation started with the increasing automation of libraries in the United States. New opportunities occurred and thus further standardization was necessary. The MARC-II format became the basic instrument for the exchange of all machine readable bibliographic information among organizations. This has subsequently led to other cooperative interinstitutional efforts, including the realization of LSP (Linked Systems Project).

The introduction of the fundamental standards mentioned above made possible more high-level cooperation. Bibliographic input tasks would be no longer unnecessarily duplicated, collection building could be done cooperatively, and enhanced bibliographic access through resource sharing could be realized. Users benefit immensely from such standardization work. On the one hand the standardized formats allow them to locate quickly the needed information, on the other hand the delivery of the documents is assured in most instances.

A number of organizations have successfully implemented bibliographic standards. The Library of Congress (LC) plays a major role in the creation and control of the bibliographic information. More specifically, LC has primary responsibility for generating descriptive data, and also for the maintenance of the authority lists for personal authors, corporate authors, uniform headings, and subject headings. Bibliographic utilities, such as OCLC (Online Computer Library Center), RLIN (Research Library Information Network), and WLN (Washington Library Network), insure nationwide access to collections' resources. Funding and national policy making are major tasks of the Council on Library Resources (CLR). The American Library Association (ALA) significantly stimulates standardization and other cooperative initiatives.

PROSPECTS FOR COOPERATION IN EUROPE

The American model for interinstitutional library cooperation conveys important dimensions of service which European nations must move toward. Progress in Europe has been slow for a number of reasons. The most obvious difference consists in the fact that the basic working conditions in Europe are much more complex than those in the USA. Europe is composed of many different countries, each representing even more distinct cultures and languages. As a result, there are many obvious differences, and fewer apparent similarities. In Belgium, for instance, there are three autonomous communities: the Dutch, the French, and the German one. The diversity in languages and administrative structures has repercussions on the interlibrary cooperation, even within this single country. Imagine, then, the difficulty of developing common standards as a basis for cooperation among many ethnocultural populations. Nevertheless the establishment of a basis for more efficient cooperation evolves. The progressive implementation of standardized working methods paves the way to this advancement. The evolution of the normalization efforts for the different activities can be summarized as follows:

CATALOGUING RULES

Cataloguing records consists of both descriptive elements and authority data. As we all know it is the latter which is of primary importance for document access. With regard to the former (descriptive) aspects, the European libraries share common conventions: the ISBD (International Standard Bibliographic Description) guidelines. But in the more important dimension of the cataloguing code, different rules coexist. Until now no normalization efforts at the international level take place. Those libraries who attempt to achieve some degree of uniformity apply a more or less adapted form of the AACRII rules. Due to the minor importance of the descriptive elements there are few chances that this uncoordinated situation will change fundamentally in the future.

AUTHORITY DATA

Uniform authority data are vital because of their critical role as the access keys to our collections. Consider, for instance, the situation of a library patron in Venice, Italy, who wants to undertake a known author search. We take Italy as an example, because it is one of the European countries with a nationally planned cooperation program. He would first consult the local database under the author's name. If he is not satisfied, his request would next be sent to the planned national Servizio Bibliotecario Nazionale (SBN) network. If there is still a need for subsequent searches, the European network has to be consulted. Such an investigation, of course, can only be completed successfully if a minimum of standardized information is available in the authority files of all the databases linked at the national and international levels.

Some international standards and "pseudo-standards" do exist for the creation of uniform author, publisher, and title entries. The most important norms are the Paris Principles. However, this effort in international cataloguing guidelines fails to affect the choice of access points and the structure of the catalogues. Further, the authority data being very culture sensitive material, the AACRII cannot serve as a European standard. In addition the multilingual dimension is important in the context of a generalized access to the bibliographic records.

Future cooperation, however, will require a solution of this dilemma. The answer lies in the establishment of standardized rules for authority data, while at the same time flexibility has to be kept. For instance, for each name, at least one normalized form or one unambiguous identification number will have to serve as a common element between the national and local systems in order to identify the corresponding records in a distributed database system. The elaboration of such a cooperative project would be a well fitting responsibility project for the respective National Libraries.

Similarly, there is a tremendous diversity in the area of subject authorities. Some countries made an effort towards national standardization. In Great Britain, for example, a new system of controlled indexing vocabulary, PRECIS, has been developed. In France, an offspring of LCSH, called Rameau, is used. Unfortunately, not all countries have forged a national policy for the normalization of subject access. Most libraries in Europe still rely on particular in-house subject indexing systems, which only amplify the already existing complexity of the problem of the multiple languages. Since the implementation of OPAC facilities, we know that efficient subject access is a matter of priority.

The creation of a brand new multilingual, controlled indexing vocabulary for all European libraries is not feasible. The solution of the subject access problem depends on the translation into the different languages of an existing and sound subject heading system. The LCSH, for example, could serve as a basis for the dialogue between the distributed databases constituting a decentralized "European bibliographic database." The English heading or an unambiguous identification number could become the normalized access key. For the creation and the maintenance of the multilingual subject authority file a centralized control is a primary requirement. One European organization has to get the responsibility for this new system.

Of course on a longer run adequate techniques for natural language subject indexing and retrieval will be developed. Because of the multidiscipline character of the material handled, and because of the multilingual context the obstacles to overcome are enormous although.

COMMUNICATION STANDARDS

For the exchange of machine readable bibliographic data, a standardized format is required, as the one existing in the USA, namely MARC. In Britain, the exchange norm has taken the form of BNB-MARC. Other countries have followed in devising other variations of MARC. The growing number of MARC-versions, of course, has not stimulated cooperation. In response, the International Federation of Library Associations (IFLA) established a new international standard, the UNIMARC format, which has not yet been widely adopted. However, recently among the European Communities, there has been growing interest in looking into the feasibility of a common use of UNIMARC. The increased need for more collaboration in Europe has to make this new international effort successful.

SYSTEMS INTERCONNECTION

Interlinked computer-to-computer communication is the final purpose of European library cooperation. Once again, in this field, normalization is the key to success. Several countries started initial work in this direction. Italy, for example, uses the Standard Network Architecture (SNA) to link heterogeneous library systems for the present and plans to migrate towards Open Systems Interconnection (OSI) in the future.

On an international level, the situation is more complex, but we can at least hope that the OSI protocols, as defined by the ISO (International Standard Organization), will produce the so needed standards to stimulate machine interworking. Currently the definition of the specifications for the interlibrary loan (ILL) and the search and retrieval (SR) library functions is reaching a final stage. The urgent pressure for more cooperation and also the danger of an uncontrolled proliferation of isolated library networks prove to be an effective stimulant for this action. For instance, the European ILL project, Interlibrary OSI Network (ION) sponsored by the Commission of the European Community, prepares the implementation of an OSI-ILL protocol between three partners: PICA in the Netherlands, Laser in the United Kingdom, and DPDU (Direction de la Programmation et du Développement Universitaire) in France. This important international cooperation effort shows that European library cooperation is both feasible and necessary.

REQUIREMENTS FOR EUROPEAN LIBRARY COOPERATION

Although several important initiatives have improved international library relations, much work remains to be accomplished. National cooperative programs (like the SBN in Italy) have emerged in several European countries and must be linked. National libraries will become the primary resources for record creation and maintenance. Also the promotion of national and international cooperation and standardization will become one of their primary duties.

Concerning the access to the documents, guidance through subsequent channels will have to be provided: first the local facilities then the national network and finally the "European Library." An efficient coordinating body will be needed in order to well orchestrate the multiple new tasks. Organizations like the Commission of the European Community, EFLC (European Foundation of Library Cooperation), ELAG (European Library Automation Group) and LIBER (Ligue des bibliothèques Européennes de recherche) will continue to stimulate the realization of new cooperative programs. A progressive restructuring of the national organizations will take place and a supranational component will be added.

The development of an infrastructure for cooperation is an essential but difficult task. The necessity, however, justifies the effort. Efficient bibliographic access is a primary requirement. Thus it is our responsibility to find ways to better serve library patrons in a world more and more based on the values of information and knowledge.

Several of the ideas expressed in this paper have been presented in a more detailed way at different international conferences.[2,3,4]

REFERENCES

1. [Iljon, Ariane.] (1987) "Plan of action for libraries in the EC: First draft for discussion." The Commission of the European Community. DG XIII. 22 pp.
2. Goossens, Paula. (1990) "The European Library: A Summing Up." In: Bibliographic Access in Europe, edited by Lorcan Dempsey, pp. 289-303. London, England: Gower Publishing Company Ltd. (Paper given at the 1989 Bath Conference.)
3. Goossens, Paula. (1990) "Multilingual Bibliographic Access Via Subject in Europe." Paper given at the "European Conference on Library Automation and Networking," Brussels, Belgium, 9-11 May. 9 pp.
4. Goossens, Paula. (1990) "Libraries in Europe: Future prospects." Paper given at the 36th National Conference of the "Associazione Italiana Biblioteche," Venice, Italy, 26-29 September. 9pp.

NATIONAL DEVELOPMENTS IN INFORMATION AND COMMUNICATION TECHNOLOGIES

Bibliographic Access in the United Kingdom: Some Current Factors

Philip Bryant

SUMMARY. This paper describes three of the most important factors in the current provision of bibliographic access in the UK: the national bibliographic service; bibliographic standards and the booktrade; networking. These factors are considered against the background of the CEC DGXIIIB *Plan of Action for Libraries in the EC*.

The author is conscious that a stimulus to the production of this 'special issue' was provided by the First International Conference on Bibliographic Access in Europe[1] arranged by the Centre for Bibliographic Management (CBM) at the University of Bath in Sep-

---

Philip Bryant is Director, Centre for Bibliographic Management and the UK Office for Library Networking, The Library, University of Bath, BATH, BA2 7AY, UK.

© 1992 by The Haworth Press, Inc. All rights reserved.

tember 1989. The conference was organised around four themes: stand-alone and public interactive library systems, centralised databases and cooperatives, networks and networking, and bibliographic standards. It is self-evident that these themes were not mutually exclusive. This paper is based on three main topics which similarly interact and together they cover a major part of the same spectrum of interests as that discussed at the Bath conference, but, this time as related to the UK. They are:

- the national bibliographic service;
- bibliographic standards and the book-trade;
- networking.

In 1985 a Resolution (85/C271/01) of the Council of Ministers of the European Commission established the overall aims for the *Plan of Action for Libraries in the EC*[2] published by the Directorate General XIIIB of the Commission of the European Communities (DGX-IIIB) in 1987. In order to provide itself with as much background information as possible for determining the Plan's priorities, DGX-IIIB commissioned a study in 1986 referred to in short as LIB-2. LIB-2 consisted of a series of national surveys by each of the 12 member states. The UK report *State of the Art of the Application of New Information Technologies in Libraries and their Impact on Library Functions in the United Kingdom*[3] was prepared by the Library Technology Centre at the Polytechnic of Central London and the Library Association and submitted to the CEC in November 1986. This report was the most comprehensive of its type produced in the UK to that date. The Centre for Catalogue Research (as CBM was then called) contributed to the report by undertaking a study of the UK's main machine-readable catalogues. For those wishing for a detailed description of the use of, and planning for, information technology in libraries in the European Community, the twelve reports[4] are indispensable reading. An update of the 1986 data, once again commissioned by DG XIIIB, is currently being undertaken and, as before, the Bath Centre is collaborating with the Polytechnic of Central London in its preparation.

There was a great deal of enthusiasm in the UK when the Plan of Action was first launched and there was maximum cooperation in connection with LIB-2, but recently there have been signs of disappointment that progress has not been as speedy as some had hoped. Nevertheless, whatever the merits of the arguments of critics, and the feelings of frustration, there can be no doubt that the CEC's initiatives—both the LIB-2 study and the Plan of Action—provided a considerable stimulus for the library community. In fact it can be argued that for the UK the Plan has already been a positive success because of the cooperative attitude it has inspired between many British librarians and their colleagues in mainland Europe; even if this has not always resulted in actual projects. In any case, apart from the international dimension, the Plan has almost certainly encouraged the adoption of a more all-embracing view of technological developments and their effective implementation. Five 'action lines' were defined and Action Line 1 was concerned with two main topics: national bibliography and retrospective conversion and Workshops on these were convened by DGXIIIB at Luxembourg in 1990. Both topics are of considerable interest to the UK library and bibliographic community which has made a significant contribution to the debate.

Computerised bibliographic systems should never be considered separately from the data to be handled by those systems. Technology on its own is patently useless. It is there to store, manipulate, transmit and provide access to data, and no technology, however brilliant, can adequately recompense for absent, inadequate, or poorly defined data. Ensuring that bibliographic data is present when required, is adequate and is properly defined, lies at the very heart of good bibliographic control and of the problems facing the world's national bibliographic agencies; not least the British Library National Bibliographic Service (BLNBS).

THE NATIONAL BIBLIOGRAPHIC SERVICE

In the UK the political and economic situation of recent years has meant that the pressures of resource allocation have been an ever present fact of life. There are limits, both locally and nationally, to the investment which can be made in meeting the requirements of bibliographic control; however, problems of providing a timely, cost-effective service that meets national and international needs are not only experienced by the UK, but by many others in the international bibliographic community. This was made very clear in an article by Hope Clement of the National Library of Canada.[5] Hope Clement was writing as Chair of the International MARC Network Committee (IMNC) which in 1988 had decided to survey the record creation processes of its members within the context of Universal Bibliographic Control (UBC). The conclusions of the survey mirrored so much of the UK situation:

> Human resources and budgetary constraints are seen as the greatest problem in the production and delivery of national bibliographic products and services. These must be coupled with increasing publishing volumes. All national libraries surveyed have had to function in an environment of restraint in which resources have decreased at the same time as the demand for library services has increased, both in volume and complexity . . .
> Problems commonly identified were delays in the receipt of acquisition of the national publishing output, especially at the legal deposit stage; increasing backlogs, due to publishing increases and the addition of new forms of material; the long and highly complex bibliographic record creation process, especially authority work; the requirements to use several complex bibliographic standards . . . the need to follow revisions to standards which are consistently changing . . . "

By the mid-1980s the British Library's (BL) backlog of uncatalogued items required for the national bibliographic service had risen to over 40000 and was continuing to grow. Despite much effort by the British Library Bibliographic Services (BLBS) the 'hit rate' for UK MARC records had remained stubbornly low. This 'hit-rate,' which has been monitored by CBM since January 1980, measures the percentage of UK MARC (now BNB MARC) records available at the time they are required by the library community for cataloguing new books. Between 1981 and 1985 it hovered between 59 and 64 per cent. A target was set for the BLBS within the BL's first five-year strategic plan[6] to increase the 'hit-rate' to 85 per cent by 1990. (This figure was ambitious and, for a number of reasons outside the control of the BL and which will not be explored here, unattainable.) In order to reduce the backlog, and to deal with the rapidly increasing output of titles published in the UK, decisions were taken to reduce by half the costs of current record creation by the BLBS.

In July 1987 the BLBS reviewed its policies and issued a consultative paper entitled *Currency with Coverage*[7] which provided for:

a. The introduction of AACR2 Level 1 description for 50 per cent of BNB MARC records. The categories of material proposed for this treatment were modern English fiction, children's books, items with 32 pages or less, and works on science, technology and religion.
b. The discontinuation of Library of Congress Subject Headings (LCSH) except for names.

Currency with Coverage stated that:

> BNB MARC records are intended to support effective and efficient book selection and acquisition, information retrieval, cataloguing and other technical processes, and to do this they must have the three qualities of accuracy, consistency and timeliness.

Of these qualities improved 'timeliness' was undoubtedly the main aim of *Currency with Coverage* and the 'hit-rate' rose significantly. It now averages over 80 per cent for academic libraries, over 70 per cent for public libraries and the overall combined average is 77 per cent. At least half of the improvement can be attributed to the new policy; however, other factors also played a part such as the significant improvement, which occurred at the same time, in obtaining better performance from publishers providing input to the Cataloguing in Publication (CIP) programme. CIP is the bedrock of BLNBS record creation.

There is no doubting the importance of 'timeliness.' Centralised cataloguing has always had one major drawback and that is the delay which all too often occurs in creating and delivering records to libraries. This delay impedes good library management and costs money—the very opposite to the aims of centralised cataloguing.

The significant increase in the number of integrated library systems (ILS) with their associated 'acquisitions' modules means that the bibliographic records needed in order for them to operate are required at a much earlier stage than hitherto. The slow delivery of records by the BLBS had become critical by the mid-'80s and there was a good deal of concern expressed at a national level because the situation was affecting scholars, library suppliers, and others in the book world in addition to librarians.

Despite the foregoing comments there are many in the UK who are convinced that fullness of bibliographic 'description' and 'heading' is all important and that quality cataloguing demands this feature even at the expense of 'timeliness.' A response to the new BLBS policy stated that "timeliness was less of a consideration than good quality records" — by which was meant 'full' records. This was a view expressed in a number of other responses received; nevertheless, there is a marked divergence of opinion over what is meant by a 'full' catalogue record. With the development of OPACs, and the provision of networked access to them, more and more searches are being conducted at a distance. The requirement is increasingly for annotatory detail to tell searchers what items are about, rather than for traditional bibliographic description such as detailed pagination.

In addition to reducing the level of bibliographic description for the specified categories of material the subject indexing policy was revised and as from January 1991 the BLNBS is introducing a new subject system to replace PRECIS. COMPASS (Computer Aided Subject System) uses the basic components of PRECIS while dispensing with the latter's complex coding. This should simplify the indexer's task and so speed the throughput of records.

The BLBS has had the problem over the years of being both the provider of the national bibliographic record and at the same time a competitor in the market place and attempting to square the circle has proved difficult. In the UK there was a general recognition that the difficulties being faced needed constructive discussion between all sectors of the library and book-trade community. A major seminar entitled Bibliographic Records in the Book World: needs and capabilities[8] held at Newbury in November 1987 will be referred to later. A second complementary 'forum' was organised jointly by the Library Association and the MARC Users Group (MUG) on The Future of a National Database.[9] At the end of two days of lively discussion an attempt was made to reach a consensus. The following statement received general support:

> We recognise that the national bibliographic effort exists on two levels:
>
> a. the creation of the national archival record for which the focus and responsibility lies with the British Library, as advised by the library community;
> b. the development of a network of databases from which users can be satisfied for various functions, the coordination of which may lie with the British Library, but the responsibility for which should be more widely shared.

Later in 1988 it was recognised that assistance would be needed by the BLNBS if it was to be able to provide the records for the national imprint required by the UK library community. A suggestion had been made a little time before that the five other libraries entitled to receive legal deposit copies of books published under UK copyright should also be able to provide records to the BLNBS. In February 1989 the BLBS announced that "the Librarians of the six UK copyright deposit libraries were planning a cooperative programme in the creation of bibliographic records for the British National Bibliographic Service."[10] A pilot project was implemented in the autumn of 1990 and at that time they started "contributing an agreed range of records to the BNBMARC file; those records will be appearing in tape, online and CD-ROM products and services from January 1991."

Mr. Peter Lewis retired as Director General of the BLBS Division in April 1989 and the NBS became one of three directorates created out of the reorganisation of the Division. The NBS consists of two groups: Market & Support and Planning & Standards. Market & Support is responsible for the printed *British National Bibliography* (BNB) and the British Library Automated Information Service (BLAISE). *BNB on CD-ROM* was launched in the middle of last year. There are two distinct products—a backfile 1950-1985, and a current file, 1986 to date.

A project of particular interest within the European context is the 'National libraries project on CD-ROM.' A comprehensive description is given in a recent article by Robert Smith.[11] January 1990 saw the beginnings of an initiative by seven European national libraries following a pilot CD-ROM project undertaken jointly during 1988/89 by the BL and the Bibliotheque nationale. The project is part-funded by the CEC and aims to encourage the exchange of bibliographic records in Europe and results will include prototype software for linking CD-ROM products to other applications, e.g., local library systems.

Bibliographic Standards and the Book-Trade

Because libraries' automated systems now require bibliographic records at as early a stage as possible there is a growing readiness in the UK to take records from a variety of sources, and book-trade sources are becoming very important in this respect. In turn the book-trade is increasingly concerned with its own need for timely, effective bibliographic records and the publication and implementation of *Currency with Coverage* resulted in criticism from the trade as well as from libraries. The fact is that the whole pattern of record creation in the book world is changing. As Lorcan Dempsey has pointed out: "Many publishers now form part of large communications organisations. There is growing awareness of the importance to the trade of information technology for the dissemination of bibliographic information especially in the export market where British books are competing with other English language publications for sales."[12] A leading export bookseller at the 1987 Newbury seminar Bibliographic Records in the Book World remarked that the lack of records in a UK catalogue database could lead to UK booksellers losing sales. The dilemma is that the lack of a record may be due either to slowness in its production, or to perceived paucity of content leading to it not being selected for inclusion in the database.

In addition to a mutual concern about issues relating to timeliness and content of records, libraries and the book-trade have had a growing and converging interest in electronic data interchange. This has led to a spirit of cooperation between the UK library and book-trade communities of recent years which has been impressive. A particular impetus was given to this cooperation by a one-day conference entitled Electronic Transmission Standards in the Book World[13] held in London in October 1986. Because of its sub-title, "Avoiding an Electronic Babel," this conference became known as the 'Babel Conference.' David Whitaker reported that there was "overwhelming agreement at the meeting that the progress towards more and more rapid electronic communication in the book world would be facilitated by agreement on common standards for the messages which are transmitted."[14] As a result of an initiative taken by MUG, in response to this call for action, the Book Trade Electronic Data Interchange Standards (BEDIS) Committee was established. The membership represented library cooperatives, public and institutional libraries, the BLBS, library suppliers, booksellers, publishers, service suppliers, systems suppliers and the Article Numbering Association (ANA). BEDIS split its work into interest areas and five small Working Parties were established:

WP1 : Publishers Bibliographic Databases
WP2 : Short Title Records
WP3 : Commercial Messages — orders
WP4 : Sales Data
WP5 : Standard Address Numbers

BEDIS's initial report was published in 1988 as a Discussion Paper. Among its findings was that MARC was the most widely used standard for storage and transmission of bibliographic data throughout the world's libraries, and it was recommended that MARC should be adopted as the standard for 'bibliographic data' for all parts of the book-trade. Work would be undertaken to establish what amendments were required to the standard so that it would be hospitable to extended use. TRADACOMS (Trading Data Communications), suitably adapted for the specific needs of the book-trade, was recommended as the format for 'commercial' messaging.

The Book Trade Electronic Communications Committee (BTECC) was set up in 1988 by the Councils of the Booksellers Association, the Publishers Association and the Library Association to "encourage and facilitate progress on standards which would increase the efficiency of electronic communication between the constituent parts of the book world." BTECC took over responsibility for BEDIS, the latter acting as BTECC's technical Working Party. The two committees are now to merge to form the Book Industry Communication (BIC) Group with its initial funding supplied by the three sponsoring associations and the BL. BIC's immediate role is the further implementation of the BEDIS recommendations.

The results of the second stage of BEDIS's work were reported at Babel II held in London in October 1989. Some minor amendments to the reports of the BEDIS Working Parties were made in the light of consultation at this conference and also as a result of comments received from other referees. The final report[15] of the BEDIS Working Parties was published on behalf of BTECC in April 1990. It is the report of Working Party 1 on Publishers Bibliographic Databases which is of most relevance to this article. The Working Party identified data elements which it recommended to be mandatory for publishers' systems, and data elements which it identified as highly desirable. It recommended the building of interfaces between publishers' bibliographic databases and the requirements of MARC, and that MARC be extended to accommodate new data elements which were identified. The Working Party expressed its willingness to negotiate with the British Library for the necessary extension of the UKMARC standard and to negotiate with system suppliers for the building of the interfaces required by its recommendation.

More and more there has been talk in the UK of the need for bibliographic record supply to be regarded as a 'continuum' from the publishers to the end user. It is considered that this continuum should, as nearly as possible, extend from the time a new title is a scribbled note on an editor's desk to the time the relevant record is used by a bookshop, or consulted in an OPAC. As the BEDIS final report pointed out; "the application of a common bibliographic standard along that continuum must result in economies for all concerned." However, it is rare for publishers in the UK to have their own established computerised bibliographic databases — notable exceptions are Oxford University Press and Pergamon Press — but in 1987 Book Data was set up. Book Data is an independent UK company which was established to meet the needs of publishers, booksellers and their customers for product and market information through a computer database. Book Data's services are subscription-based and a full database of a subscribing publisher's current and forthcoming titles is created in order to provide a variety of services, e.g., publishers' catalogues, 'fliers,' housekeeping data. For subscribing booksellers, selective information services are provided to help with more effective marketing. The goals set by Book Data include: systematic creation of fully descriptive records; interconnection of bibliographic and non-bibliographic information; dynamic updating; a multi-purpose, multi-product system. The very full records which can include short and long abstracts and contents page-data, maintains a considerable level of compatibility with UKMARC practice and the intention is that this compatibility should become even closer. "Once a record of this kind becomes available, backed up by a clearinghouse which takes responsibility for its consistency, its regular updating, and its distribution to the user community, it can be used as source material for many other purposes."[16] Book Data records have been used for BL CIP; for *British Book News* entries; for entries of educational books into the National Educational Resources Information Service (NERIS) and they are currently being used in an OPAC research project undertaken jointly by the Centre for Bibliographic Management and City University entitled 'Improving online access to bibliographic records by enriching the records with subject-descriptive material derived from machine readable book trade data.' Book Data records are now available for consultation through OCLC's EPIC service.

The problems encountered in the UK over the past years in ensuring an adequate supply of bibliographic data has resulted in a number of library suppliers such as John Menzies Library Services (JMLS) creating major databases of their own and becoming closely involved with discussions regarding such matters as the MARC format, AACR2, record quality, subject processing and more.

It is quite clear that the use of booktrade databases of all types is increasing throughout Europe. In the UK one which is especially important, and which has a long history, is that of J. Whitaker & Sons. Responsible in the UK for the Standard Book Numbering agency, Whitaker has published *The Bookseller* and *British Books in Print* for many years. In 1986 a CD-ROM version of the latter was produced and in January 1988 Whitaker launched their BOOKBANK CD-ROM Service which is produced monthly and lists some 450000 titles in print, plus recently 'out of print' titles, from over 12000 British publishers. It has proved to be a very successful venture. Recently Whitaker was awarded the contract to produce CIP records for the BLNBS as from the end of 1991. The new contract will provide for the supply of advance information in MARC format for 30000 titles a year.

Networking

In the UK the development since 1984 of the Joint Academic Network (JANET), an X-25 packet-switched network with gateways to other academic networks—especially in Europe and North America, is having a considerable impact on the academic library world and beyond. Peter Stone has described the existing and potential library use of JANET[17] and Lorcan Dempsey has written a major report,[18] specially commissioned by the British Library Research and Development Department (BLRDD), on changes in the way libraries are using networks to deliver services to end users, and to communicate between themselves and other organisations. Certainly the growing network infrastructure is a major new factor in the provision of bibliographic access, whether for the purpose of record retrieval and supply, document delivery or in the provision of remote access to OPACs and other databases. The implications within the total European context are far reaching indeed.

At present the OPACs of some 60 universities and other academic and research institutions can be consulted over JANET, but probably the most significant development in the use of the network for the provision of bibliographic access has been that of CURL (Consortium of University Research Libraries). In 1987 the libraries of the universities of Cambridge, Edinburgh, Glasgow, Leeds, London, Manchester and Oxford established, with the aid of funding from the then University Grants Committee, a pilot project for resource sharing over JANET. The aim was to facilitate the exchange of information about library acquisitions and holdings, and to arrange for the exchange of catalogue data between member libraries. This database of some 2000000 records, but many fewer titles, includes only the current MARC cataloguing of the participating libraries. Now that the period of the original grant has expired the member libraries may fund the project themselves, but, if so, what the exact conditions and provisions for its future use would be is not known to the author at the time of writing.

An initiative has also been taken regarding the UK book trade's potential use of JANET. A meeting held at Aston University in September 1990 discussed ways of encouraging greater use of data exchange to support book and serial supply and to encourage formats which are independent of specific vendors. Some initiatives for investigation were identified, including a small study to develop an operational requirement for library systems, and a survey of attitudes to innovative services such as direct ordering and e-mail announcements. It was hoped that these would be funded within the near future.[9]

Because of the bourgeoning of interest, and the plethora of activities, the JANET User Group for Libraries (JUGL) proposed to the BLRDD in 1989 that a focal point for networking was urgently required by the UK library community. The UK was in advance in its use of wide area networks, (WANs) and public telecommunication networks, but libraries required a more coordinated approach to their effective use. To this end the UK Office for Library Networking (UKOLN) was established by the BLRDD for an initial period of three years to work under the auspices of CBM. UKOLN's primary goal as announced in December 1990 is "to enable the production of common or cohesive strategy for the use of networking by the UK library and information community." The aim is to enable the community itself to produce this strategic plan by April 1992. In order to achieve this a series of highly focused workshops on specific areas of use of networking by libraries were held during 1991. The reports and recommendations produced by each of these workshops have provided the framework for the final national strategy document.

REFERENCES

1. *Bibliographic Access in Europe: First International Conference:* the proceedings of a conference organised by the Centre for Bibliographic Management and held at the University of Bath, 14-17 September 1989; edited by Lorcan Dempsey (Aldershot: Gower, 1990).

2. *Plan of Action for Libraries in the EC* (Luxembourg: CEC DGXIIIB, 1978).

3. *State of the Art of the Application of New Information Technologies in Libraries and their Impact on Library Functions in the United Kingdom* (London: Library and Information Technology Centre, 1987).

4. *State of the Art of the Application of New Information Technologies in Libraries and their Impact on Library Functions* — EUR report (EUR 11036) 12 vols/29 microfiches.

5. Hope Clement, "National Bibliographic Agencies Cataloguing Survey," *International Cataloguing and Bibliographic Control* 19(January/March 1990): 6-10.

6. *Advancing with Knowledge: the British Library Strategic Plan 1985-1990* (London: British Library, 1985).

7. *Currency with Coverage*. Consultative Paper (London: British Library Bibliographic Services, 1987).

8. *Bibliographic Records in the Book World: Needs and Capabilities*. Proceedings of a seminar held on 27-28 November 1987 at Newbury; compiled by Derek Greenwood — (BNBRF Report 33) (London: BNB Research Fund, 1988).

9. *MARC Users' Group/Library Association Forum on the Future of a National Database*, [a Report] (London: MUG/LA, 1988).

10. *British Library Bibliographic Services Newsletter* 48 (February 1989): 2.

11. Robert Smith, "National Libraries Project on CD-ROM," *Electronic Library* 8 (December 1990): 412-414.

12. Lorcan Dempsey, "*Bibliographic Records: Use of Data Elements in the Book World*" (Bath : Bath University Library, 1989).

13. *Electronic Transmission Standards in the Book World*: Avoiding an Electronic Babel. Report of a one-day seminar held 15th October 1986 (London: BNB Research Fund, 1986).

14. *BEDIS Discussion Paper* (London: J. Whitaker & Sons Ltd., 1988).

15. *BEDIS Report of the Working Parties of the UK Book Trade Electronic Data Interchange Standards Committee on: Publishers' Bibliographic Databases; Electronic Orders; Standard Address Numbers; Short Title Records, and with a Paper on the Electronic Collection of Sales Data* (London: J. Whitaker & Sons Ltd for BTECC, April 1990).

16. David Martin and Mike Vernon, "BOOK DATA: The Design and Development of a New Kind of Bibliographic Database" In: *Bibliographic Access in Europe* op cit.

17. Peter Stone, "*JANET: a Report on its Use for Libraries*" (London: British Library Research and Development Department, 1990).

18. Lorcan Dempsey, "*Libraries, Networks and OSI: A Review with a Report on North American Developments*" (Bath: UK Office for Library Networking, 1991).

19. *Library Association Record* 92 (December 1990): 884

London and South Eastern Library Region (LASER)

J.M. Plaister

SUMMARY. The London and South Eastern Library Region (LASER) is an organisation for *Library Cooperation*. Its objects are the improvement of library facilities available to the public by the promotion of cooperation between libraries and other organisations. Co-operation maximises the use of scarce resources both of stock and staff expertise. Computer technology and extension into networking has allowed LASER members to make economic and multiple use of bibliographic records as well as stocks of books and periodicals. The use of internationally recognised standards also makes links with other cooperative organisations a practical possibility.

PURPOSES

The London and South Eastern Library Region (LASER) is a focus for library co-operation in London and South East England. It is part of a nationwide system for regional library co-operation and financed, as are all the English Regions by its member libraries. Its objects are the improvement of library facilities available to the public by the promotion of cooperation between member libraries and other bodies within and outside the area of the region having functions in relation to libraries. Membership is open to *all types of library*.

LASER has access to the 70 million or so volumes in the stock of member libraries for interlending, photocopying and reference. Its union catalogue contains entries for 3 million titles, 2.5 million of

---

J.M. Plaister is Director of the London and South Eastern Library Region (LASER), 33/34 Alfred Place, London WC1E 7DP, United Kingdom.

© 1992 by The Haworth Press, Inc. All rights reserved.

which are recorded in machine-readable form and maintained in an online minicomputer system.

It has fiction in English, and less-used foreign languages are available through special collection schemes. Self-sufficiency in British books is assisted by a subject specialisation scheme maintained by the public libraries in the area.

LASER makes serials accessible through the maintenance of a regional union catalogue of periodicals, at present maintained manually and unpublished. Catalogues of playsets and sets of music scores which can be obtained through the interlending system are available for use. LASER libraries have collections of audio-visual material which can also be accessed.

LASER locates and arranges loans of books and other library materials for libraries and their users. If items are not available for loan or photocopy within the membership of the region, the search can be extended to libraries outside the membership and area of the region, including the British Library.

LASER undertakes bibliographic research and identification of items on behalf of its members. It also deals with requests from its members for subject- or topic-based access services, which range from speculative searches for specified items to requests for factual information.

By pioneering the production of microfilm listing of International Standard Book Numbers (ISBN) and British National Bibliography (BNB) serial numbers and library locations, LASER encourages direct interlending between libraries.

LASER operates an interlibrary *transport scheme* and has a contract with the British Library Document Supply Centre (BLDSC) to carry items to its users in the LASER area.

By its computer and communications system (*VISCOUNT*) LASER can offer online access to its machine-readable database for interlending and stock purposes, and this online facility is now used by almost all LASER area public libraries. Online access is also available as a result of the VISCOUNT projects to locations in the East Midlands, West Midlands, North West and South West Regions, the National Library of Scotland Lending Services and Yorkshire and Humberside Joint Library Services.

LASER staff have carried out extensive research into the use of public videotex for community information provision through libraries.

Through the conversion of its union catalogue into machine-readable form, LASER can provide entries for machine-readable catalogue (MARC) and extra-MARC items recorded in the catalogue, and the LASER staff can advise through their own experience and research on the development of automated library systems, including the use of MARC.

It provides *training courses* for staff from member libraries on the techniques of interlibrary lending and bibliographical research. Staff are also available to organise seminars and courses for groups of librarians in the area either alone or in cooperation with BLDSC on the resources available outside their own libraries.

LASER organises a co-operative acquisition and cataloguing service for material in the five major Indic languages (CILLA) and produces a quarterly booklist and MARC tapes of this material. It has also developed cataloguing and transliteration rules for this material, suitable for public libraries.

HISTORY

Although formal regional library cooperation had existed in the South East of England since 1928, LASER itself was established as a result of an amalgamation between the London Union Catalogue (LUC) and the South Eastern Library System (SERLS). This merger was proposed by the 1961/1962 Working Party on Interlibrary Cooperation in England and Wales and took place in 1969.

LUC, established in 1929 by the London metropolitan borough libraries, and SERLS, established in 1933 and covering the South East excluding London, each maintained union catalogues of library locations used for interlibrary access and loan.

The introduction of a computer-based system was the direct result of the amalgamation, which aggravated the problem already existing in the former organizations of an annual intake of notifications to the union catalogue, unmanageable by traditional methods without a substantial and expensive increase in staff.

In April 1986, LASER became a *non-profit company limited by guarantee*, as well as retaining its *charitable status*. Further changes may need to be made to enable further capital investment in the necessary automated activities, in the light of government legislation over the years.

Following research sponsored by LASER, the next three largest library regions (North-West, South-West and Scotland), the British Library and British Telecom, the Viewdata and Interlibrary Systems Communications Network (VISCOUNT) was established in the 1980s. The project has successfully implemented a policy for bringing all major users of LASER online from 1st April 1988, and providing a framework for extension of an online interloans system throughout most of the UK as we move into the 1990s.

ORGANIZATIONAL AND NETWORK STRUCTURE

LASER is governed by a Library Council, the members of which are nominated and elected in accordance with the membership of the region. An elected Management Committee controls day-to-day operation, working through various sub-committees.

The activities of the region and the money needed to operate it are determined by the Council on the advice of the Board (Management Committee) and the Director/Company Secretary.

DATABASE

There are some 2.5 million records on the LASER minicomputer system, representing the 70 million volumes held in member libraries. The database is a union catalogue of bibliographic records, all of which are held in a single file available for online interrogation. The system provides access to the following bibliographic data:

- UK MARC (BNB) 1950 to date (complete file)
- LASER Retrospective extra-MARC post 1900, authors A-HO
- LASER extra-MARC current 1977 to date (complete)
- Library of Congress MARC for books acquired by LASER libraries
- Whitaker records for books acquired by LASER libraries

- BLDSC monograph holdings information and records since 1980
- Library locations for libraries in LASER
- Library locations and extra-MARC entries for EM,NW,SW, WM, Scotland and Yorkshire regions
- OCLC records for books acquired by SW and Scottish regions 1988-

HARDWARE CONFIGURATION

The VISCOUNT system comprises:

- AEG Modcomp Tri-D 9740 minicomputer
- 3 Gigabyte disk subsystem
- Magnetic tape subsystems
- 8 VDUs at LASER HQ
- 48 port communications subsystem
- 1 Trend system console
- Gandalf PACX 2000 data switch with 2 VDUs for console/logging
- 20 rackmounted Jaguar Quartette/Dowty Mayze 24 intelligent modems (V21/V22/V23/V22bis with ARQ and MNP Level 2 error correction)
- 5 IBM-compatible PCs, printers and 2 standalone modems

There are 60 remote user sites. Region HQs in Bristol, Manchester and Edinburgh have two or three PCs each linked by Kilostream 9600 digital leased lines to London. Other region HQs have a single PC. Individual libraries have a single PC, usually a colour system with hard disk, printer and intelligent Quartette modem, controlled by a *specially configured PC software* package supplied by LASER which may be used for other purposes in addition to VISCOUNT. A few users have other microcomputers emulating videotex terminals as a low cost option.

TELECOMMUNICATIONS

The network uses multi-speed asynchronous dial-up lines, normally at 2400/2400bps with error-correction. Remote users may use British Telecom's GNS X25 service, either through the Dial 1 service using BT PADs, or private PAD connected via X.25 leased line to PSS. At present only region HQs use the Kilostream digital service leased lines, but for maximum reliability, additional leased lines are being considered as a future enhancement.

SOFTWARE AND FILE STRUCTURE

The VISCOUNT system is now based on Informix relational database software running under REAL/IX, Modcomp's enhanced version of Unix System V.3, together with the Ceemore electronic mail package. This replaced an earlier proprietary database from Real Time Control of Watford, running on a Data General Nova minicomputer. Bibliographic records are maintained in a single database.

LASER also has a Modcomp Viewmax/Viewtracs videotex system, currently used mainly for information and directory information.

FUNCTIONS AND SERVICES

Online

Known as VISCOUNT since 1986, the system is designed to facilitate interlibrary lending of known items, although it can also be used for bibliographic checking and reference work. The system provides access to the records in the database by the following modes:

- Author (including added entries and cross-references)
- Title
- Acronyms for Combined author/title, Author and Title

- Book number (ISBN, BNB, LC, OCLC, BLDSC or VISCOUNT record number for extra-MARC material)
- Date
- Dewey classmark

A simple *"acronym"* or bibliographic search key is used to speed searching. This method has been found to be quick, easy to learn and use and specific enough to eliminate excessive duplication on retrieval in a database of over two million records. Where several records do exist for a single search key, matches are listed for selection and display. The system displays the *bibliographic data in MARC format or 1580 long- or short-form displays*, then the *locations* for an item. In addition, single or batch-mode changes can be made to the location data by member libraries from remote terminals. Staff at region HQs in London, Bristol, Manchester, Birmingham, Leicester and Wakefield and at the National Library of Scotland Lending Services in Edinburgh can also create extra-MARC records online and amend location information. Catalogued items can also be reviewed and amended by the chief cataloguer online prior to transfer of the new items into the main database. The database is archived to Video 8 cartridge tape daily.

Once an item is found by a user on the database, it can be requested electronically using the messaging service, which is part of the system. Messaging is a *store and forward mailbox* system, enhanced by a real-time link to the bibliographic database to allow automatic insertion of bibliographic data in requests and full audit trailing of chargeable British Library loan forms and VISCOUNT request forms, the numbers for which are supplied automatically by the system. Mail may be sent to other users, or to BLDSC's *ARTTel (Automated Requests Transmission by Telecommunications)* system, using a single user interface. The central system supports the application by providing the VISCOUNT Transaction Store (VTS) to allow automatic forwarding of requests, replying, chasers and progress checking. Viewdata 86 services provide a library directory and status information, interloan and information technology news and routine statistics of British Library interloan form usage. *Microcomputer terminal* systems allow automated fetching and printing of mail, storing and processing of incoming and outgoing messages and convenient and rapid access to library status and help information while on- or offline.

Offline

Updating is the main batch operation, performed regularly to regenerate indexes. At each update, records are loaded from external magnetic tapes (e.g., BNBMARC) as well as from internal temporary holding files. Tapes of location information from member libraries are loaded bimonthly after preprocessing at a bureau to merge and validate the data. Location amendments performed online are, however, active immediately, and constitute the majority of such processing.

Other batch operations, including catalogue production if required and selective record services with tailored or standard formats are performed using a duplicate database held on a bureau mainframe and cross-updated by magnetic tape.

COOPERATION WITH OTHER SYSTEMS, DATA EXCHANGE

The LASER database contains British National Bibliography records purchased in the form of weekly BNBMARC magnetic tapes. Some LASER members also submit magnetic tapes to notify LASER of additions and withdrawals. LASER then uses the union file to generate COM-fiche catalogues, since 1988 as a backup to the online system, before then to allow direct interlending. LASER is also working with the other major library automation cooperatives in the UK and overseas, to improve library computer facilities.

A *VISCOUNT Steering Group* has been established to advise on further automated network development, with representatives from all participating regions and the British Library.

COSTS OF DEVELOPMENT AND MAINTENANCE AND FUNDS

All development, maintenance and funds are obtained from members and those taking LASER services. The only grants received from outside bodies have been for research. Currently, six regions outside the LASER area have a few sites each connected to VISCOUNT, and these are charged special provisional rates pending future enhancement of the network, expected in the 1991-2 year.

MEMBERS, USERS OF NETWORK, USERS COSTS, MEMBERSHIP FEES, USERS INSTRUCTIONS

In 1989-90 (latest figures available), 548,543 LASER region location updates were implemented on the VISCOUNT database, plus some 450,000 from three other regions. Members handled 194,646 requests for interlibrary loans. Thirteen thousand requests per month were being handled by the VISCOUNT online messaging system by April 1990, when LASER had some 59 members, plus around twelve other VISCOUNT users.

Subscriptions to each service are fixed annually. Instruction manuals are issued for all services, i.e., interlibrary loans, transport system (LASER operates a fleet of 17 vans to move interloan packages between members and BLDSC), VISCOUNT online system, etc.

FUTURE PLANS

Upgrading of the VISCOUNT network will be completed early in 1991, to provide improved searching, processing and communications links. Additional libraries have been invited to join the expanded network.

LASER is keenly involved in the development of suitable international and national standards for computerised library work, particularly interlibrary loans. It has carried out work in collaboration with similar agencies in other countries towards the creation of an *open systems interconnection (OSI)* network to support an international interlending system in Europe. A pilot/demonstration project *(Project ION)* is being undertaken with France, the Netherlands and the Commission of the European Community.

The participants in the project are:

- London & South Eastern Library Region(LASER) in the UK
- Pica Centrum voor Bibliotheekautomatisering in the Netherlands
- Ministère de l'Education Nationale, Direction de la Programmation et du Développement Universitaire, Sous-Direction de Bibliothèques (SDB) in France

The major objectives of the project are:

i. to achieve interconnection between three computerised library networks in the United Kingdom, in the Netherlands and France in order to support and develop international interlending and messaging services
ii. to improve the efficiency of international interlending services
iii. to demonstrate the capabilities of OSI communication protocols in a message-oriented environment for interlending services in the interconnection of computerised networks with different technical characteristics.

The project, which started on 15th February 1990 will last three years, is being co-financed by the participants and the Commission of the European Communities (DG XIII B). The total cost of this development is 2,579,000 ECUs.

Three phases of development are planned:

i. the specification of technical, functional and service requirements for the interconnection of three interlending networks
ii. the implementation of operational testing of the 051 communications based ILL system

iii. the use and evaluation of the system by forty-six libraries in the UK, the Netherlands and France.

Phase 1 of the project has been successfully completed. It has been reviewed by a panel of independent experts and the European Commission has given the go-ahead for the next two phases of the project.

The next phase will convert the specifications and concepts into a practical pilot service. It will cover the procurement cycle, installation, setting to work and training requirements needed to introduce the users to the service.

The stage is then set for phase 3 of the Project ION, which will be the use and evaluation of the pilot system by forty-six libraries in the UK, the Netherlands and France.

CONCLUSIONS

Self-sufficiency is difficult in good times; in lean times it is impossible. It makes sense to co-operate with other libraries.

Co-operation maximises the use of scarce resources both of stock and staff expertise.

Computer technology and extension into networking allows for economic and multiple use of bibliographic records as well as stocks of books and periodicals.

Access to Information in the Nordic Countries

Antti Soini

SUMMARY. This article concentrates on the national services and databases in the Nordic countries. The availability of information via networks is the main discussion topic. The Nordic libraries have a long tradition of cooperation. The basic idea at present is to make the national information of each country available to all users within Scandinavia, to create a "Union Nordic Library." The necessary qualifications for that kind of co-operation are very good: the development of the national systems is in process or already operational at a high technical level; the Nordic research networks are connected to each other and to international networks; the data itself is in standardized form and very well covers the recent publications.

GENERAL TRENDS

During the past couple of years the European Community (EC) has launched a long-term plan which can be called "The European Library." The idea of the project is that the information in European libraries should be made available to all users via networks as easily as using the local library. A Plan of Action for Libraries has been published and widely discussed at European library conferences. The plan is structured into five action lines, addressing the core action areas: source data, the interlinking of systems, new services for users, the development of new tools and facilities for library staff and, finally, the exchange of expertise, support for other lines of action, feasibility studies, etc. Concrete projects to support these themes have been solicited.

Antti Soini is Director, Automation Unit of Finnish Research Libraries, P.O. Box 312, 00171 Helsinki, Finland.

© 1992 by The Haworth Press, Inc. All rights reserved.

The Nordic countries have been actively participating in the European library community efforts and have very closely accommodated their functions to the general rules, standards and practices. We have also taken one step further in the Nordic countries: the cooperation between the libraries moved onto a practical level long ago. The basic idea is, however, the same as for the European Plan of Action: to make the information available to all users, to create a "Union Nordic Library." As a matter of fact "The Union Nordic Library" already exists as a network, even though much work remains to be done to get more information, more services and more users attached to it. The basic mission of "The Nordic Library" or, rather, of a Nordic information network is to get the national database services of each country created and used.

On the next few pages, I will concentrate on the national services and their availability via networks. Some aspects of national coordination efforts in the area of library automation in general are also included. Many services and databases are bypassed in this condensed description. For those needing more detailed information or practical advice, the addresses of key institutions are attached. The situation described conforms to the state of development in March 1991.

DENMARK

Libraries in Denmark have selected or created their own local automated systems, shared systems, therefore, are very few. A variety of systems and computer brands are represented. On the national level there is a governmental body, Statens Bibliotekstjeneste, which coordinates the library and information field. It has a separate office, FEK (Forskningsbibliotekernes Edb-kontor), which develops and supports central automated library services. This central organization has been used as a consultant by the major libraries to ensure that a basic compatibility is achieved between the local system and the central bibliographic services.

One of the major national projects during recent years has been to make the library databases available via DENet. DENet is the university and research network in Denmark, which uses the common TCP/IP protocol for communications. A special menu for libraries,

FIND, gives access to about 15 databases directly via DENet at the moment. Both central and local library databases are included.

The most important central databases available via the FIND-menu are the union catalogue and the national bibliography databases:

ALBA is the Union Catalogue database, consisting of about 2 million records with library codes attached and as many without library codes, which are used as a bibliographic pool. The Danish National Bibliography is also searchable in ALBA but only for domestic research libraries. ALBA database is hosted by FEK.

SCANNET is a guide to databases in the Nordic countries, a small but very useful database especially for those who do not know where to look for what in Scandinavia.

Via FIND you can also access several local library databases:

ALIS the database of the technical libraries and institutes, hosted by Danmarks Tekniske Bibliotek,
REX the database of the Royal Library in Copenhagen,
AUBOLINE Aalborg University Library database,
RUBIKON Roskilde University Library database, etc.

DENet is connected to other Scandinavian university networks and international networks as well. Access to Danish databases connected to DENet is therefore technically very easy. The policy of charging and passwording varies.

The information itself is easily available in Denmark, and the coverage of the data is good. DENet allows an easy access to this information within the country and from abroad.

For more information: Forskningsbibliotekernes Edb-kontor (FEK)
Nyhavn 31 E,
1051 Copenhagen, Denmark

FINLAND

Co-operation between libraries has been and still is a predominant feature in Finland. Since 1974 there has been a national body for the co-ordination of library automation, The Automation Unit of Finnish Research Libraries (TKAY), at the Ministry of Education. At its initiative and effort a batch-based cataloguing system was implemented in 1978, and a separate online information retrieval system has been available since 1980. At present there are 1.2 million online searchable records in these national databases:

KOTI   the National Bibliography database 1967- , (also available on CD-ROM),
KAUKO   the Union Catalogue of foreign monographs,
KATI   articles in Finnish periodicals,
KAUSI   periodicals database
MUSA   sound recordings published in Finland, etc.

These so-called KDOK databases are available through the MINTTU information retrieval system of the State Computer Centre. The English commands of MINTTU usually conform to the CCL, with which most information specialists are familiar.

A totally new co-operative project, LINNEA (Library INformation NEtwork for Academic libraries), started in the mid-eighties. According to the plan, the same local library system should be installed at each of twenty university libraries. These systems should be connected into a single, uniform network, into which national bibliographic resources and services will also be integrated.

The keystone of this plan is the uniformity of the data and the system software at all sites including the central national databases like the National Bibliography and the Union Catalogue. This kind of central co-ordination was only possible with governmental funding by the Ministry of Education.

Selecting the software vendor was a long and arduous process. Finally in 1988 the contracts were ready for signing with the American company, VTLS Inc. At the moment about ten university libraries have their VTLS systems installed and running. Planning for the central system configuration and services has started, and the installation of the union catalogue database is scheduled for 1993.

The central system will mainly be used for shared cataloguing and authority control, interlibrary loans and information retrieval. Also foreign MARC records can be added for use as a bibliographic pool.

The local VTLS systems are connected to the local area networks of the universities. FUNET, the Finnish University and Research Network, connects the university LANs using the TCP/IP protocol. The capacity of FUNET allows the local library systems to join the network as a part of the normal communications between the universities. FUNET has also established connections with the Scandinavian, European and worldwide research networks. Therefore, there are no technical obstacles in accessing any university library using VTLS from almost anywhere in the world. When the central system database is loaded in 1993, this opportunity will be even more attractive for users needing information on Finnish literature or on publications at Finnish libraries.

For more information: Automation Unit of Finnish Research
Libraries (TKAY)
Teollisuuskatu 23-25
00510 Helsinki, Finland

ICELAND

Iceland is a very small country, about 250,000 inhabitants, half of them living in the capital Reykjavík and its surroundings. In a modern country of that size, the availability of information within the country is really not a problem at all.

The two largest research libraries are the National Library and the University Library. Almost all the other research and special libraries are situated in Reykjavík or in its close vicinity, too.

As the country is small, research is very much dependent on the availability of information from abroad. Therefore, there is great interest in telecommunications in Iceland. SURIS, the Association for Research Networks, is an organization consisting of nearly all publicly funded research institutions and academic schools in Iceland. SURIS runs and administers the national network, ISnet, which has connections to other Scandinavian and worldwide research networks. Of course, X.25 networks are also available via the local PTT. Both interlibrary loan requests and online retrievals from abroad are widely used in Iceland.

Is it possible to access Icelandic databases from abroad? At present there are no bibliographic databases available via networks. The Union catalogue of periodicals in Icelandic libraries is in printed form and produced by the National Library. The Icelandic National Bibliography has been automated since 1979, but it is published in a printed version only.

However, when the commercial integrated library systems are fully implemented, the situation will undergo a rapid change. At the moment two of them are already in use in Iceland. DOBIS/LIBIS, the IBM based library system is used by the Reykjavík city library and its branches and also by the Medical Library of the Central Hospital. These installations are very recent ones (since the beginning of 1990) and not yet fully used.

The National Library and the University Library (which will be consolidated in the near future) have selected the British system LIBERTAS, running on VAX computers. This system has been experimentally used since June 1990. The system will be fully implemented in phases over the next three years. According to the plans, the system will eventually incorporate the Union catalogue and the National Bibliography. Thereafter, access to Icelandic publications as well as publications in Icelandic libraries, will be available also to foreign users via the ISnet network.

For more information: University Library
                        101 Reykjavík, Iceland

NORWAY

In Norway two paths of parallel development have been formed. The University Library in Oslo, as a national library, has concentrated on bibliographic databases, services and standards. The BIBSYS system, developed by the Computing Centre at the University of Trondheim, has created a shared system for local library use. The university libraries have all united to use the BIBSYS system, in the other libraries a variety of domestic and foreign small library systems are used.

Services by the University of Oslo Library (UBO)

Several online databases are available with a total of two million records to be searched. There are two sets of databases available, each of them with its own search system: UBO:BOK and TRIP.

The most important UBO:BOK databases are:

SAMBOK the Union Catalogue for monographs in about 300 Norwegian libraries,
BOK the National Bibliography (1971-),
NOTA Norwegian Periodical Articles (1980-),

Databases BOK and NOTA are also available on CD-ROM consisting of the National Bibliography records 1962-1990. An equivalent disc is also planned for the union catalogue records.

In the TRIP system there are more than twenty databases. Most of them are quite small and equivalent to special collections at UBO. The biggest TRIP databases are:

LC87-89 Library of Congress records 1987-89
SAMPER Union Catalogue for periodicals in Norwegian libraries.
NOSP Union Catalogue for periodicals in Nordic libraries.

The Norwegian research and university network, UNINETT, is connected to other Scandinavian and international research networks. It makes all these databases available both locally and internationally.

A new service has also been implemented recently: ordering copies of articles via the SAMPER database. This service is based on telefax services, but it can also be used via the electronic mail of the UNINETT.

BIBSYS

The development of the BIBSYS started as early 1972 at the Computing Centre of the University of Trondheim. The first releases of the acquisitions and search modules were made in 1975 followed by other functions. With new functions new libraries joined the system, and now there are ten participants. The system is centralized and uses an IBM main frame. The database includes more than one million records.

A new period of development has recently started, and the aim is to implement a new BIBSYS-III by mid-1993. The architecture will be changed to a more distributed one. The local functions will be run on local computers, but the union catalogue database will be maintained centrally. The system will be based on the UNIX operating system and other open standards.

The present BIBSYS-II system is also open to external users either via DATAPAK (X.25), a dial-up connection or through the INTERNET (TCP/IP). The user may choose to search the whole database or the logical part that belongs to one participating library. It is also possible to search the pool of external MARC records of the Library of Congress or the Norwegian National Bibliography.

For more information on
National services: University of Oslo Library
                        Planning Department
                        N-0242 Oslo 2, Norway

BIBSYS: BIBSYS
                        N-7055 Dragvoll, Norway

SWEDEN

In Sweden the central library system LIBRIS (LIBRary Information System) was established at the beginning of the seventies. Originally it was a Union Catalogue database only, but since about 1980 it has also included the data of Swedish National Bibliography. In the mid-eighties local, integrated library systems were introduced to the Swedish market and the state of automation can now be described as central bibliographic databases combined with local library systems.

From the networking point of view the situation is quite complex. Many different library systems on various computer brands are expected to communicate with LIBRIS. There are eight different local systems installed at eighteen university or research libraries. The central system, LIBRIS, runs in an IBM environment. Until now the Swedish university and research network, SUNET, has not been used by the local library systems, and the LIBRIS computer is not yet connected to SUNET, either. However, there are plans to expand the capacity of SUNET, and a decision to connect the LIBRIS IBM mainframe to the TCP/IP-based SUNET network has been made.

To minimize the problems of many different local environments, the LIBRIS organization has developed PC-based communication software which makes it possible for the user to switch between the central and the local catalogue just by pressing function keys. The communications are particularly problematic because of the huge character set (about 400 characters) used in LIBRIS cataloguing records.

What are the services of the LIBRIS central database? In the first place it is used for shared cataloguing. Thirty-five libraries are updating the central database online, and there are different ways of downloading the records back online or offline. The database contains approximately 2.5 million records. The database can also be used as a union catalogue for searching and for locating interlibrary loans. The LIBRIS catalogue contains not only the union catalogue for research libraries and the Swedish National bibliography but also records from the Library of Congress and from the British Library. These records can be used both for searching and cataloguing purposes. When the records are transferred to the local catalogue, they are converted into LIBRISMARC format (at the cost of about 40 cents per record to outside customers). No library has found it worthwhile buying and converting foreign records on their own account, even if they have the facilities available to do that. There are about 500 libraries in Sweden and the Nordic countries having dial up access to the LIBRIS database for searching purposes.

Access to the information in the LIBRIS system covers the libraries and their users in Sweden very adequately. When LIBRIS is available via SUNET, access will also be easier for the Scandinavian and international users. The database itself is large, representative and up-to-date. The LIBRIS system is the responsibility of the Royal Library.

For more information: The Royal Library, LIBRIS department
P.O.Box 5039
102 41 Stockholm, Sweden

CO-OPERATION IN SCANDINAVIA

Owing to geographic and cultural conditions, the Nordic countries have very intensively and closely co-operated also in the library field. This has been also organized at the governmental level since 1977 when NORDINFO, the internordic body promoting, supporting and co-ordinating the co-operative projects on libraries and information access, was established. NORDINFO is financed by the Nordic governments and has a permanent office in Helsinki, Finland.

Library conferences and meetings on general or specific topics are frequent and regular. In Scandinavia, it is also natural and easy to contact colleagues and friends outside meetings to tell news, ask for advice or to discuss new ideas. This kind of unofficial co-operation is often used (and was needed to obtain information for this article, too).

Some practical results of Nordic co-operation can be mentioned here. There are a Nordic Union Catalogue for Periodicals (NOSP) and several Nordic bibliographies and databases on specific topics. One of the most recent co-operative products is IANI (Intelligent Access to Nordic Information Systems). IANI is a PC-program which, with one log-on procedure and one command language, gives access to different databases on different hosts in the Nordic countries. The IANI-project is funded by grants from NORDINFO.

The state of information access in the Nordic countries is at a high technical level, the co-operation between the Nordic countries and Nordic libraries is very close. The networks already make it possible to access and browse a great amount of national and local databases. The year 1993 seems to be the next great milestone in many of the Nordic countries, when especially interesting things will happen: in Finland the central system of the LINNEA network will be established, in Iceland the bibliographic databases will be made available, in Norway the BIBSYS III will be implemented with its local and central databases. This will be a challenge to develop Nordic co-operation further, a challenge which we will gladly meet.

APPENDIX

DELTAGARFÖRTECKNING

Ageberg, Marianne
Alzén, Anne-Marie
Ask, Nina
Bergqvist, Berit
Bergstedt, Cecilia
Blomberg, Håkan
Blomqvist, Karin
Eklund, Anders
Eklund, Margareta
Fallberg, Inga
Gustafsson, Ingela
Gustafsson, Ingegerd
Hellström, Christina
Karlsson, Boel
Kindenberg, Birgitta
Klingberg, Christer
Koldenius, Malin
Lindblom, Kerstin
Molin, Brita
Lundell, Hans
Nilsson, Sören
Olsson, Britt-Marie
Persson, Annika
Sebeniusson, Ingrid
Serrander-Jansson, Monica

APPENDIX (continued)

Svensson, Karin
Taylor, Helesine
Thyresson, Göril
Wallén, Christina
Wilhelmsson, Wivianne

Förhindrade att närvara vid första träffen:

Berit Bergqvist   kommer, men ngt försent
Margareta Eklund
Göril Thyresson   kommer fredag fm
Monica Serrander   kommer lördag

DEVELOPMENTS AND IMPLICATIONS OF ONLINE EUROPEAN DATABASES

Access to European Online Databases

Erwin K. Welsch
Eleanor Rodini
Victoria Hill

SUMMARY: Describes access to European online databases and their capabilities. Databases covered include FRANCIS, a French database covering the humanities, the European Communities Databases, and the German national bibliography as an example of the humanities and social science databases offered by STN. The authors conclude that these databases have potentials for providing new information possibilities to students in European studies but that their utilization presents implementation problems that are unlike those found in other online databases.

Libraries have, since the mid-1970s, successfully implemented access to a steadily increasing number and variety of online services of bibliographic and other information. Reference librarians have overcome problems such as the multiplicity of command language

Erwin K. Welsch, Eleanor Rodini and Victoria Hill are affiliated with the Memorial Library, University of Wisconsin, Madison, WI 53706.

© 1992 by The Haworth Press, Inc. All rights reserved.

structures and the technical difficulties in moving from the use of terminals to the implementation of microcomputers, and have used these new capabilities to develop high levels of information services for their patrons.

The implementation of access to European databases and online services provides potentially new opportunities for service to patrons in the humanities and social sciences whose primary research or scholarly interests are Europe. Databases produced in Europe can supplement such databases as *Historical Abstracts* and the *MLA International Bibliography* that include European-language materials and offer more comprehensive coverage of bibliographic information.

Librarians in the Memorial Library of the University of Wisconsin-Madison have been working with three of these services in an effort to determine the applicability of these online titles to the needs of scholars in the humanities and social sciences concerned with Western Europe. The following describes work with the "FRANCIS" database by Eleanor Rodini; the European Communities databases by Victoria Hill; and the German national bibliography provided through STN by Erwin K. Welsch and illustrates the potential of these services but also some of the problems that reference librarians might encounter in using them.

SEARCHING THE FRANCIS DATABASE

In 1987 I learned that the French-produced database, FRANCIS, was soon to become available to computer searchers in the United States through TELESYSTEMES-QUESTEL, on its new software, QUESTEL-PLUS. An acronym for "French Retrieval Automated Network for Current Information in Social and Human Sciences," FRANCIS would offer our faculty and students access to computerized information in such fields as ethnology and ancient history, disciplines that are unavailable on American systems. At the time I attended the QUESTEL-PLUS training session, in 1987, FRANCIS had not yet been remounted on the new software and the "FRANCIS User Manual," dated 1980, was intended for an earlier command language. When I learned that FRANCIS was finally available on QUESTEL-PLUS, in 1989, I began experimenting with the database, relying, however, on scanty and out-of-date documentation. Despite occasional frustrations, the results of these searches were frequently rewarding and I hope that this article will inspire greater interest among searchers in this country.

FRANCIS is produced by the French Institut de l'Information Scientifique et Technique (INIST). Prior to 1988 the activities of INIST were carried out by two separate documentation centers: the Centre de Documentation Scientifique et Technique (CDST) and the Centre de Documentation Sciences Humaines (CNRS). FRANCIS is one of the approximately 70 databases available through the French online retrieval service QUESTEL, Inc, which became a separate division of TELESYSTEMES S.A. in 1990. The original company, TELESYSTEMES-QUESTEL, was created in 1979 under the auspices of the Mission Interministrielle pour la Diffusion de l'Information Scientifique et Technique (MIDIST). Although based in Paris, QUESTEL maintains an office in Falls Church, Virginia. In 1982 QUESTEL signed a cooperative agreement with IST-Informatheque, Inc. of Montreal, Canada, making its databases available to Canadians. The increased usage of QUESTEL in Canada seems to have indirectly benefitted U.S. users by bringing staff to the Falls Church office who are more familiar with FRANCIS, although none seems to have had actual searching experience with the database. To date, in fact, I have encountered no one who has searched FRANCIS.

QUESTEL, however, is not unknown to American searchers. In a series of three articles published in *Online* in 1986, Marcia Olmsted and Sylvie Labrèche compared in great detail the software of DIALOG Version 2 and QUESTEL-PLUS.[1] Their purpose was to highlight the improvements in both systems brought about by the new software enhancements. In doing so they have provided a good overview of QUESTEL-PLUS, a system that combines some of the advantages and even the command language of DIALOG and BRS, but that has the annoying disadvantage of WILSONLINE in that continuous printing is not possible. It is not my purpose here to discuss the command language of QUESTEL-PLUS; one feature, not covered in the Olmsted-Labrèche article, deserves mention, however. This is the truncation symbol " + ." The " + " symbol retrieves all documents containing the designated root of the term, regardless of the number of following characters, and, unless instructed to do otherwise, displays the resulting list. In other words it corresponds to the EXPAND or ROOT command of DIALOG or BRS. In attempting to search a database with outdated documentation, foreign-language descriptors, and no thesaurus, this feature has proved invaluable.

FRANCIS (see Figure 1) is actually a multiple database, consisting of 20 subfiles. Sixteen of these correspond to the variously numbered bibliographies, entitled *Bulletin Signalétique*, which are published by the Centre de Documentation Sciences Humaines. Coverage, for the most part, begins in 1972 and is international in scope. According to a recent INIST brochure, English language documents outnumber those in French in half the subfiles; other languages are well represented, however.

FRANCIS includes citations to journal articles, books, book reviews, conference reports, and other scholarly publications, and almost all records (see Figure 2) include a very short abstract. Searches may be limited to a particular document type, as well as to a particular language. Most of the files are updated quarterly, but there is often a considerable time lag between the date of publication and the date of entry in both the database and in the printed bibliographies.

Within FRANCIS the subfiles are known as "chapters" and may be searched separately or in any combination, either by preceding the search with a LIMIT command (e.g., . . . LIM 523 /CH) or by "ANDing" search results with the chapter number, which is the same as the number of the corresponding printed *Bulletin* (e.g., Sicily AND 521 /CH, that is, *Bulletin Signalétique 521: Sociologie-Ethnologie*). In addition, each subfile is assigned to a particular subject area and may be searched individually by entering the appropriate French term in the /DO field (e.g., Ethnologie /DO). A list of searchable fields is shown in Figure 3.

The subfiles and the bibliographies on which they are based have a classified arrangement and can be searched by the classified section numbers within the "Chapter" field (e.g., 521.VI /CH, that is, the religion, magic, and witchcraft section in the ethnology chapter). These same section numbers may also be searched by using standardized terms in French in the "French generic descriptors" field (e.g., sociologie de l'education /FG) or in English in the "English generic descriptors" field (e.g., sociology of education /EG). However, in order to search by section number or to use the FG or EG fields, it is necessary to consult the "Plans de classement des publications de FRANCIS," the classification schemes of the subfiles published by CDSH in 1985.

In addition to the broad subject categories described above, each document is assigned subject descriptors. In theory there are both English and French descriptors; however, I have found a good number of records that have only French descriptors. Since the subfiles are produced by different research centers, there is no thesaurus for the database as a whole. According to a brochure put out by CDSH is 1988, it was possible to buy a "Guide thématique" for 15 of the subfiles. However, when Memorial Library ordered two of these in 1989, one was out-of-print and the other was not yet published. I recently wrote to INIST and learned that there are now "Lexicons," that, is "alphabetical lists of terms used to index the information in the database," for four of the subfiles and "Thesauri," that is, "lists of terms used to index the data bases and organized on the basis of a semantic or hierarchical relationship" for three of them. The exact difference between these is not clear to me, but they are now on order. I also learned that there is now a 1989 edition of the "FRANCIS User Manual," which we have also ordered.

Even without a thesaurus, it is possible to achieve good results searching FRANCIS, especially if one uses the truncation character, "+." My very first search was for a faculty member looking for articles on the Roman cult of the emperor. I entered the term "cult+" and some 100 terms later stumbled on "culte imperial," with 67 citations found for the phrase (see Figure 4).

A search using the English word "cult," "ANDed" with "emperor OR imperial OR caesar," produced only 14 hits. Keyword searching with the various positional operators provided by the QUESTEL-PLUS software is also possible. In fact a keyword search using French terms retrieved 98 citations for the search subject just mentioned.

Using the "+" character is essential when doing an author search. Only initials are used for first and middle names and name

FIGURE 1

Content of a reference :

A reference includes the document's title, author(s), language, identification number, date of publication, type, field, abstract, descriptors, classification code, classification scheme chapter and location.

	Online since	Number of updates/year	Number of references as of 1.1.1989	number of references added/year	languages of documents indexed			Type of documents indexed (%)		% of fully analysed documents
					French	English	Others	Journal articles	Books, reports, dissertations, proceedings, etc.	
FRANCIS (Computerized bibliographic research file containing news and information from the fields of Humanities and Social Sciences)										
ART AND ARCHEOLOGY (Near East, Asia, America)* (526)	1972	4	33,800	2,800	28	44.5	27.5	93.5	6.5	97
INTERNATIONAL BIBIOGRAPHY OF ADMINISTRATIVE SCIENCE (528)	1972	4	60,200	4,200	78.5	10	11.5	79	21	87
ETHNOLOGY (529)	1972	4	51,100	4,100	36.5	42	21.5	86.5	13.5	70

Database	Year								
HISTORY OF SCIENCE AND TECHNOLOGY (522)	1972	4	74.600	23.5	43	33.5	87.5	12.5	55
HISTORY OF LITERATURE AND LITERARY SCIENCES (523)	1972	4	96.500	26.5	40	33.5	97	3	75
HISTORY OF RELIGION AND RELIGIOUS SCIENCES (527)	1972	4	155.800	32	29	39	93.5	6.5	92
INFORMATION TECHNOLOGY AND THE LAW (603)	1974	2	7.100	55	25.5	19.5	57	43	100
PHILOSOPHY (519)	1972	4	83.600	15	46	39	98	2	60
PREHISTORY AND PROTOHISTORY (525)	1972	4	55.200	36.5	26	37.5	88.5	11.5	65
INDEX OF ART AND ARCHEOLOGY	1973	4	197.400	16.5	24.5	59	66.5	33.5	68
EDUCATIONAL SCIENCES (520)	1972	4	94.600	35	45.5	19.5	90.5	9.5	60
LINGUISTIC SCIENCES (524)	1972	4	62.500	25.5	47	27.5	90	10	31
SOCIOLOGY (521)	1972	4	72.700	33.5	48	18.5	87.5	12.5	80
DOGE (Management) (616)	1980	2	9.200	78	22	0	15.5	84.5	100
ECODOC (General Economics) (617)	1981	4	10.300	82.5	8.5	9	64.5	35.5	100
ENERGY ECONOMICS (731)	1972	4	30.500	37.5	52	10.5	63	37	100
EMPLOYMENT AND TRAINING ** (600)	1974 to 1984	4	10.000	85.5	11	3.5	55	45	100
RHESUS (Health-related Humanities) (610)	1978	4	13.100	84.5	15	0.5	81	19	100

FIGURE 2. A Sample FRANCIS Record

```
?..li max

 1/16 - (C) CNRS-FRANCIS
 NO   : 87-523-03326
 DO   : LITTERATURE
 AU   : MARCHAND (J.-J.)
 TI   : Ecriture et pouvoir a la Renaissance italienne in Travaux de la
         section d'italien de la Faculte des Lettres de l'Universite de
         Lausanne.
 SO   : Etudes de Lettres; CHE; 1984; no 4; pp. 3-16
 DT   : PERIODIQUE; P
 LA   : FRE
 DP   : 1984
 CH   : 523.III
 CC   : 523.198
 FG   : Histoire de la litterature
 EG   : History of literature
 FD   : Pouvoir politique; Convention litteraire; Italie; Renaissance; Siecle
         15-16; Bruni (L.); Machiavel (N.); Arioste (L. 1'); Tebaldeo (A.);
         Bembo (P.); Aretin (P. 1')
 ED   : Political power; Literary convention; Italy; Renaissance; Century
         15th-16th; BRUNI (L.); MACHIAVELLLI (N.); ARIOSTO (L.); BEMBO (P.);
         ARETIN (P. L')
 AB   : L'etude des rapports entre ecriture et pouvoir chez L. Bruni,
         Machiavel, l'Arioste, A. Tebaldeo, P. Bembo et l'Aretin fournit une
         clef d'interpretation unique pour des oeuvres apparemment differentes
         et permet d'expliquer la maniere dont un ecrivain reutilise ou
         transforme des codes litteraires
 LO   : CDSH
```

forms are not standardized. Thus, a search for articles by Jean-Jacques Marchand finds entries under the following forms: Marchand (J.J.), Marchand (J.), and Marchand (J.-J.). Curiously, the double initials precede the single initial in the truncation display, while the initials connected by a hyphen follow all. In short, one must read the display very carefully to find all forms of the same name.

Another situation in which the use of the " + " sign pays off is in searches for time periods. The desire to restrict a topic to a particular historical period is common in the humanities and is always difficult to do in an online search. Some database producers, such as the Modern Language Association for its *MLA International Bibliography* and ABC Clio for *Historical Abstracts and America: History and Life,* have attempted to make such searches easier by creating special fields in which historical periods can be indicated and by

FIGURE 3

| SEARCHABLE FIELDS |

AB	French abstract
AF	Affiliation of author(s)
AM	Author (organisation)
AU	Author (person)
AUC	Author quoted
CC	Classification code
CH	Section
DO	Subject area
DP	Document publication date
DT	Document type
DTC	Quoted document type
ED	English descriptor
EG	Generic English descriptor
FD	French descriptor
FG	Generic French descriptor
LA	Document language
LO	Document location
NO	Document reference number
OD	German or Spanish descriptor
OG	Generic German or Spanish descriptor
SO	Document source
SOC	Quoted document source
TI	Document title
TIC	Quoted document title

standardizing the form of entry (e.g.: HP = 1800-1899, to indicate the nineteenth century). But in an article published in Database in 1983, James Sweetland showed that 20 different search terms had to be employed to capture the concept of "turn of the century" in *America: History and Life*.[2] FRANCIS uses the term "century" (e.g., "siècle 5" in French; "Century 5th" in English) and puts the phrases in the "descriptor" fields. However, not only is the form *not* standardized, but there are so many typographical errors or variant forms for the same concept, that a great deal of care must be used when selecting from the display generated by the truncation command. (See Figure 5.)

My searches of the FRANCIS database have been decidedly experimental in nature, hampered by inadequate documentation and by the absence of knowledgeable support from either the producers of the database or QUESTEL. Now that there is new documentation

FIGURE 4

```
?cult+

    1    1903    CULT
    2      48    CULT OBJECT
    3       1    CULT OBJET
    4       9    CULT OF THE DEAD
    5       1    CULT OF THE PAST
    6      53    CULT PIT
    7      23    CULT SCENE
    8      20    CULTA
    9       1    CULTA LATINIPARLA
   10       1    CULTANE
.......

Several screens later

    1      67    CULTE IMPERIAL
    2       2    CULTE INDIVIDUEL
    3       1    CULTE INTERIEUR ET EXTERIEUR
```

FIGURE 5

```
?siecle 5+ /de

    1    1842    SIECLE 5
    2       1    SIECLE 5 (DEBUT)
    3       2    SIECLE 5 (DEPUIS)
    4       1    SIECLE 5 - [6-06]
    5       1    SIECLE 5 A LA FIN DU MOYEN AGE
    6      99    SIECLE 5 APR. J.-C.
    7       1    SIECLE 5 APR. J.-C. (DEPUIS)   AUX YUAN
    8       1    SIECLE 5 APR. J.C.
    9       1    SIECLE 5 AUX CINQ DYNASTIES
   10       2    SIECLE 5 AV. J. C.
   11     112    SIECLE 5 AV. J.-C.
   12       1    SIECLE 5 AV. J.-C. (AVANT)
   13       5    SIECLE 5 AV. J.-C. (DEPUIS)
   14       1    SIECLE 5 AV. J.-C. A L'ISLAM
   15       1    SIECLE 5 AV. J.-C.-17 APR. J.-C.
Remaining terms: 45

    1       1    SIECLE 5 AV. J.-C.-2
    2       1    SIECLE 5 AV. J.-C.-20
    3       1    SIECLE 5 AV. J.-C.-20 APR. J.-C.
    4       1    SIECLE 5 AV. J.-C.-3
    5       1    SIECLE 5 AV. J.-C.-3 APR. J.-C.
    6       1    SIECLE 5 AV. J.-C.-3 AV. J.-C.
    7       1    SIECLE 5 AV. J.-C.-4 APR. J.-C.
    8       1    SIECLE 5 AV. J.-C.-5
    9       2    SIECLE 5 AV. J.-C.-5 APR. J.-C.
.......
```

searching should be easier, but I had to call the QUESTEL office to learn of the existence of these tools. There was no mention of them in any of the issues of the organization's newsletter, *Questel-a-Gram* that I have received. Nevertheless, I recommend FRANCIS as a database for academic libraries. Where else can one have on-line access to information in ancient history, archeology, the history of religion, or of science and technology? I would not approach a search of FRANCIS without careful preparation, nor without consulting a French dictionary; but so armed, I have been able to perform successful searches in areas of the social sciences and humanities I could not reach before.

EUROPEAN COMMUNITIES

For many years, large collections of documents from the European Community and its predecessor, the European Coal and Steel Community, lay relatively undisturbed on the shelves of the U.S. libraries collecting them. With the issuance in 1985 of the White Paper from the European Commission on "Completing the Internal Market," however, a process was set in motion that has awakened a great deal of interest in the EC even on this side of the Atlantic. The projected completion date of 1992 has assumed "near mystical and inspirational proportions," according to Ian Thomson, a British specialist on EC documentation. Publications about the EC have increased exponentially, and American scholars have begun to offer courses on the EC and 1992 and to consult the documents neglected for so long.

In addition to the extensive paper publications by and about the European Communities, the Communities have made available to the public a large number of databases that are just beginning to be tapped in the U.S. There is little information available about how much use is being made of these databases; at a meeting in Washington of EC depository librarians in October, 1990 (the first such meeting in many years), it appeared that CELEX, the legal database, is the most frequently consulted at this point in time. For potential American users seeking information beyond the user manuals distributed by the EC, there are two helpful resources of British origin available. The first is "EC Databases Column" and periodic articles addressing specific databases authored by Terry Hanson and appearing regularly in the British journal *European Access*. The second is Colin Hensley, the Database and Informatics Officer of the Delegation of the Commission of the EC in Washington, D.C. His article, "European Community Databases: Online to Europe"[3] gives a good overview of the many databases maintained by the EC, and his personal assistance can also be helpful in trying to access them.

From the point of view of the librarian serving the academic community in the U.S., the most easily accessible and perhaps the most useful databases are those available through the Eurobases host in Brussels. These databases are available free to EC depository libraries — a very important factor with limited academic budgets. User libraries need only to pay for establishing a telecommunications node and pay for telecommunications costs. There are user guides for each of the databases, and in addition the EC publishes a *Eurobases Information Bulletin* which contains information on new developments, search tips and other news items.

CELEX, the official database of European Community law, has been available to the public since 1981, and is now also part of the "Europe" library on LEXIS/NEXIS. CELEX is organized in 10 "sectors" containing a wide variety of legal materials — treaties, acts, secondary and supplementary legislation, case law from the European Court of Justice, and national provisions from member states enacted to implement EC directives. Many, although not all, of these sectors include full text. MISTRAL, the command language used in all of the databases on the Eurobases host, has been described by Colin Hensley as "not one of the more user-friendly query languages."[4] For this reason, many American users — often subscribers to LEXIS anyway — may choose that route to access these materials.

In the case of SCAD (Systeme Communautaire d'Access à la Documentation), the flexibility and speed offered by online searching is such an improvement over the weekly *SCAD Bulletin* in paper that mastering MISTRAL seems a small price to pay. SCAD is a bibliographic database and does not include full text for any of the documents listed. It includes citations to the main acts of community legislation, documents of the European Parliament, reports and opinions of the Economic and Social Committee, official publications of all the EC institutions, articles in approximately 1200 journals relating to EC activities, and statements of trade union and employer organizations. References cover 1983 to the present and updates occur weekly. The user manual supplied by the EC (including a 1988 update), a "SCAD Pocket Guide" and an article on the database by Terry Hanson in the August 1989 issue of *European Access* make searches reasonably simple.

The database contains four types of document (Community acts and related documents, official publications and public documents, articles in journals, and statements and opinions from trade unions and employers organisations). The attached reproduction of a page from the 2nd version of the *SCAD User Manual* (Figure 6) shows examples of the latter two types and gives an idea of the fields in the records. Boolean operators and proximity searching are available, as are truncation and masking. Search sets can be reviewed and combined. Searchers can limit results by publication year (using the PY field) or by language. Viewing search results is somewhat cumbersome, since you cannot specify a range of documents for display; either you must press the enter key after each record, or change the option which determines the number of lines sent to the terminal for display at one time to allow for scrolling.

Free text searching in the title and abstract fields is probably the most productive approach for most Americans doing a subject search, since the subject thesaurus (called the *SCAD Data Base List of Keywords*) is available only in French at this time. The British Association of EDC (European Documentation Centre) Librarians, which probably includes the most active group of English-language users, is pressuring the EC for an English thesaurus, which may be forthcoming. Of course free text searches too have to take into account the numerous languages included in the database. The problem of selecting the right French descriptor can be overcome by doing a search in the title and abstract fields which will lead to records that indicate the appropriate thesaurus terms for the topic. For example, a faculty member in the Political Science Department needed very recent information on the EC policy concerning aid for Eastern European countries. He was able to supply me with the term PHARE (Poland, Hungary: Assistance for Economic Restruc-

FIGURE 6

C Document

ND	:	SCD-88/19-C/2084
AU	:	Stavenhagen, Lutz G.
TI	:	Political priorities of the German EC Presidency.
SO	:	(AUSSENPOLITIK. Hamburg. Vol. 39. No. 1. 1988. p. 13-23.)
AB	:	The author presents the wide range of projects to be initiated during the German Council Presidency (implementation fo the Delors Package, realization of the Single European Act, internal market, economic and monetary policy; European Political Cooperation, the Community's external relations, environmental protection...).
CL	:	ALLEMAGNE RF;CE INTEGRATION;CE ACTE UNIQUE;CE RELATIONS EXTERIEURES;CE CONSEIL;CE POLITIQUE;CE PROPOSITIONS; PRESIDENCE;COOPERATION POLITIQUE
PY	:	1988
LA	:	DE;EN
LR	:	EN
ID	:	MF-68178
CH	:	17;18;26

D Document

ND	:	SCD-88/18-D/3077
CS	:	Association des chambres de commerce et d'industrie européennes (EUROCHAMBRES)
TI	:	Prise de position sur les transports combinés.
SO	:	(BRUXELLES. EUROCHAMBRES. Décembre 1987. 4 p.)
AB	:	Après avoir souligné la nécessité de promouvoir une politique communautaire dans le domaine des transports et de libéraliser les transports routiers, EUROCHAMBRES développe son point de vue sur les transports combinés et fait des propositions sur les infrastructures, le matériel, les services, la réglementation et le contrôle des documents.
CL	:	PARTENAIRES SOCIAUX;CHAMBRES DE COMMERCE ET D'INDUSTRIE; TRANSPORT MULTIMODAL;TRANSPORT RAIL-ROUTE;INFRASTRUCTURE DE TRANSPORT;TRANSPORTS TERRESTRES;MODES DE TRANSPORT; TRANSIT;MATERIEL DE TRANSPORT;CABOTAGE;FORMALITES AUX FRONTIERES;CE POLITIQUE
PY	:	1987
LA	:	FR
LR	:	FR
ID	:	PS;MF-68066
CH	:	28

turing), the acronym for one of the recently established aid programs. A search of the "TI" lexicon (which includes title, series title, and abstract) brought up several records. The descriptors field indicated that the terms "relations est-ouest" and "aide économique" were at least two of the appropriate subject headings for the topic, and a search of the subject headings lexicon (labelled CL or "mots-cles") yielded a useful and up-to-date list of documents and journal articles.

Three other databases are part of the Eurobases system. INFO-92 is a menu-driven service which provides up-to-date information on the measures needed to complete the single market. ECLAS is the bibliographic database of the Central Library of the European Commission. RAPID, only recently made available to the public, is an online press-release service, potentially very useful for quickly identifying the official EC position on any problem or situation, such as, for example, the war in the Middle East.

These five databases, however, although the most familiar to U.S. users and most likely to be used by the academic community and its libraries, are just a few of the many databases made available by the European Communities. A whole series of databases (approximately 23 at last count) are accessible through ECHO (European Community Host Organisation) in Luxembourg, and most of them are free to depository libraries except for telecommunications costs. The content varies from DIANEGUIDE, a directory of European databases and databanks, through BIOREP, which describes biotechnological research projects, to TED, which is the online version of the "S" supplement of the *Official Journal*. A user manual is available for the ECHO system, and a newsletter called *ECHO News* is also published bimonthly.

Finally, there are three statistical databases maintained by Eurostat, the statistical office of the EC; access in the US is through Wharton Econometric and Forecasting Associates (WEFA). According to Colin Hensley in his article on EC databases, there is no academic discount available for these, and access costs can be quite high. CRONOS contains more than 1 million macroeconomic time series covering every part of the economy and going back to the 1950's, according to the EC's Directory of Public Databases.[7] COMEXT is a database of foreign trade statistics since 1974, and

REGIO contains regional statistics about the various regions of the EC; the corresponding paper publication is the *Yearbook of Regional Statistics*.

In continental Europe, training programs for the use of EC databases have been available for some time, and in Britain, training availability seems to be increasing as librarians demand it. The addition of a database and informatics officer to the staff of the EC delegation in Washington in 1989 and the inclusion of sessions on the databases in the depository library conference in 1990 indicate that there is an awareness of a growing interest here and some attempt to meet our need for information.

THE GERMAN NATIONAL BIBLIOGRAPHY ON STN

STN is a firm best known, perhaps, for its scientific and technical databases. But increasingly it is offering access to databases of particular interest to librarians, humanists, and social scientists:

- FORIS: planned, current, and completed social-science research projects in German-speaking countries;
- INFODATA: German and international literature on information science and information usage from 1976 to the present. Citations are searchable in English and abstracts are searchable in English (65%) and German (35%);
- MONUDOC: historic preservation and the environment;
- SOLIS: German social-science and applied fields, including social history, with some abstracts and titles in English;
- SIGLE: European non-conventional (grey) literature including, since 1984, economics, social sciences, and the humanities.

In addition, the academic service at Karlsruhe offers access to a machine-readable database covering titles, largely monographs, appearing in the German national bibliography. Called BIBLIO-DATA (with a learning file called LBIBLIO), that database, with its potential for use as a substitute for the printed volumes or in ready reference applications in the field of European history, will be the subject of the following.

The BIBLIODATA file is copyright by the Deutsche Bibliothek in Frankfurt am Main, which also produces the printed volumes. Presumably the computer database is developed from the tapes used to generate the printed volumes. The normal database charge (as of January, 1991) was $107/hour plus .60 per citation for the "Default Online Display Format." As a holder of an academic account, I am able to search the database for a cost reduction of up to 80%, but am limited to after five weekdays, before noon on Saturday, and after five on Sunday. After several weeks of trying to schedule searching time to fit within those hours, it seemed to me that this type of account, while economically desirable, was unrealistic for ready reference or searching with an enduser present. Initially, the account had also been limited in the files that could be accessed, but as the STN news service reported:

> Effective March 3, 1991, you will be able to access all STN files through your academic account. The files will be available during the hours you currently access your CAS or FIZ Karlsruhe academic account. You will be charged the full price during these restricted hours on any file on which you are not currently receiving a discount.

I have not yet had time to explore what this means for me on a practical basis.

One initially frustrating difficulty had to be overcome before I could gain access. The opening screen reads:

Welcome to STN International! Enter x:x

I entered the "x" but that resulted in "SYSTEM IS DOWN" or "NO CARRIER" messages that I could only overcome after an STN staff member at the help desk pointed out that I had to type a "c" instead of an "x" since I was calling from the central time zone and had access only during restricted hours. He also noted that they were trying to have the message amended.

In testing the system I used two parts of the database: LBIBLIO, a static learning file that has a comparatively small number of entries, while learning basic search techniques; and, BIBLIODATA in response to a request for information from a post-doctoral student and a faculty member for information on resistance to the Nazis from 1933 to 1945.

As shown in Figure 7, the system uses commands similar to those found in other online databases.

As noted, Boolean commands make it possible to combine terms readily in a way comparable to other databases, although mixing German and English can have a disorienting effect, as when searching for monographs on the history of the German army.

```
=  > SEARCH BUNDESWEHR AND GESCHICHTE
    24 BUNDESWEHR
  1984 GESCHICHTE
L4  1 BUNDESWEHR AND GESCHICHTE
```

As a librarian who answers both ready reference and research questions using a variety of information services, I tend to follow Robert Wagers' "easy search" model, one in which "simple concepts can be represented with succinct phrases and a small number of synonyms."[6] Although I run the risk of missing materials, some questions are posed simply to determine whether an in-depth search is warranted. Therefore, I am particularly interested in the provision of help screens. The ones in LBIBLIO were functional but sometimes contained more information than I needed. The sample of the help screen for the "Display" function is shown in Figure 8.

FIGURE 7. Help Screen from the STN LBIBLIO File

```
-> HELP SEARCH
The SEARCH command is used to execute a search in the current file.
To use this command, enter 'SEARCH' and a query name or a logic
expression. The system will create an L# answer set containing the
results of the search.

A logic expression (profile) consists of L#s, E#s, text or numeric
terms and/or saved query names, joined by Boolean operators ('AND',
'OR', 'NOT') and/or by appropriate proximity operators or by
numeric operators (e.g., =, >, <) in numeric expressions.

The order of precedence for the execution of operators
is (highest first):  numeric operators; (W), (NOTW), (A), and
(NOTA); (S) and (NOTS); (P) and (NOTP); (L) and (NOTL); 'AND' and
'NOT'; then 'OR'.  Parentheses (nesting) can be used to modify this
order.
```

In addition to the provision of help screens, the database assists the user by prompting for responses. In displaying a set, it prompted for the type of display format and the number or range of entries to be displayed.

= > DISPLAY L5
ENTER DISPLAY FORMAT (BIB):BIB
ENTER ANSWER NUMBER OR RANGE (1):1-10

Prompts and help screens made it possible to overcome most technical searching difficulties, but, once these initial barriers had been overcome, encountered problems entering search terms. Despite familiarity with German, I made simple spelling errors which

FIGURE 8. Help Screens for Display Command

```
For more information about the DISPLAY command, enter one of the
following HELP commands at any arrow prompt (->).

-> HELP DISPLAY ACC ------- To see the record for a specific
                            Accession Number in a file.
-> HELP DISPLAY BROWSE ---- To browse through an answer set
                            without rekeying the DISPLAY
                            command before each answer number.
-> HELP DISPLAY COST ------ To see the approximate cost of a
                            session.
-> HELP DISPLAY EXPAND ---- To see the E# list from an EXPAND or
                            SELECT command.
-> HELP DISPLAY FORMAT ---- To see the user-defined display formats.
-> HELP DISPLAY HISTORY --- To see the commands used in this
                            session.
-> HELP DISPLAY L# -------- To see answers from a search.
-> HELP DISPLAY PRINT ----- To see the status of offline prints
                            requested in this session.
-> HELP DISPLAY QUERY ----- To see the definition of a query.
-> HELP DISPLAY SAVED ----- To list saved items for this loginid.
-> HELP DISPLAY SCAN ------ To scan through an answer set in
                            random order with a pre-defined
                            display format.
-> HELP DISPLAY SELECT ---- To see the E# list from a SELECT or
                            EXPAND command.
-> HELP DISPLAY SET ------- To see the SET parameters currently
                            active, changed, or set permanently.
-> HELP DISPLAY TOLERANCE - To see the tolerance in effect for
                            numeric fields available in the current
                            file.
-> HELP DISPLAY UNIT ------ To see the units in effect for numeric
                            fields available in the current file.
```

awareness of database costs—the meter running syndrome—exacerbated.[7] Ability to use the correct German-language terms and the ability to type those words correctly is a prerequisite for the database since it does not include English-language cognates. Use of a term or word known in English can be occasionally successful (searching just the word "Nazi," for example, yielded five responses in the LBIBLIO file), but thinking in English—Nazionalsozialismus instead of the correctly spelled Nationalsozialismus for the name of the ideology, for example, would yield zero responses.

```
= > SEARCH NAZIONALSOZIALISMUS
L1  0 NAZIONALSOZIALISMUS
```

Since German is a language that frequently combines concepts into longer words, spelling errors are easy to make and, as the results above show, can also be fatal. One solution is to use the "Expand" command (see Figure 9) to determine not only which other terms are available, but as an online spelling check (in which one word, E7, also seems to be misspelled, not the only instance of misspellings encountered in the database).

Figure 9 also shows the importance of truncation in searching for German terms because case endings could cause misleading results if just a word is specified.

In searching for materials for a post-doctoral student on the resistance (Widerstand) in the period from 1933 to 1945, I used the full BIBLIODATA file and found it easy to combine terms:

FIGURE 9. Use of the EXPAND Command

```
-> EXPAND NATIONALSOZ
ENTER FIELD CODE (BI): BI
E1         1       NATIONALSOCIALISM/BI
E2         2       NATIONALSOCIALISTE/BI
E3         0  --> NATIONALSOZ/BI
E4         2       NATIONALSOZIALE/BI
E5         1       NATIONALSOZIALER/BI
E6      1388       NATIONALSOZIALISMUS/BI
E7         1       NATIONALSOZIALISMUUS/BI
E8       169       NATIONALSOZIALIST/BI
E9        43       NATIONALSOZIALISTEN/BI
E10        3       NATIONALSOZIALISTISCH/BI
E11      400       NATIONALSOZIALISTISCHE/BI
E12      123       NATIONALSOZIALISTISCHEN/BI
```

= > SEARCH NATIONALSOZIALISMUS AND WIDER-
STAND
   1388 NATIONALSOZIALISMUS
   2193 WIDERSTAND
L7 270 NATIONALSOZIALISMUS AND WIDERSTAND

I could also have truncated using "?" to indicate any number of characters to the right of the word (Nationalsoz?), or "!" for one character at a designated position, or "#" for one or no characters at a designated position. The system includes both left and right truncation. Because the number of items, without truncation, was already large, I subsequently refined the search and was able to find a number of monographs specifically on the topic.

Since search terms are only in German, perhaps a good comparison is with colleagues in the sciences. In the same way as they have to enter lengthy and complicated scientific terms and formulas to search expensive databases, a searcher in BIBLIODATA could well benefit by, as the documentation itself suggests, carefully framing queries before going online. Another method could be to upload prepared searches,[8] or to enter complicated terms as "macros" in a communications program such as ProComm to avoid having to type lengthy German words or phrases while online.

The need to use German terms can also be a trap when one assumes, as during the pressure of a potentially costly or fast ready-reference search, that the database uses the same words for institutions or concepts as they are known in English. Looking for information on the European Economic Community was, even though some terms were represented in English, unsuccessful since I needed the German term for the community instead.

= > SEARCH EUROPEAN ECONOMIC COMMUNITY
   57 EUROPEAN
   20 ECONOMIC
   16 COMMUNITY
L4 0 EUROPEAN ECONOMIC COMMUNITY
   (EUROPEAN(W)ECONOMIC(W)COMMUNITY)

I also searched for an individual, Konrad Adenauer the former German chancellor, in LBIBIO, and quickly found 21 potential entries even in the limited test file. There are several display formats and here, as elsewhere in searching the database, the system prompts for a likely response.

= > DISPLAY
ENTER (L2), L# OR ?:L2
ENTER DISPLAY FORMAT (BIB):BIB
ENTER ANSWER NUMBER OR RANGE (1):1

As the following display in Figure 10 shows, the database producers have dealt with the problem of the "ü" and other words with letters with diacritics by including an "*" to show that the word has been changed from, for example, a standard German "für" to "f*uer." This is a standard throughout the database, but the number of asterisks on the page can be initially somewhat disconcerting.

In summary, I found that searching the German national bibliography online was a mixed success:

- The documentation is ample, although it currently uses examples that are primarily scientific and needs others that deal with the social science fields that are increasingly becoming part of the databases being offered;
- Technically the system is sufficiently similar to other online database searching so that learning basic searching techniques is not difficult;
- Availability of the system at limited times in exchange for a substantial discount proved to be more of a barrier than had been anticipated since it limited interaction with the user and had to be carefully scheduled;
- The need to type lengthy search terms in German could be a drawback and might require significant preparation time.

But overall I concluded that this could be an effective service if carefully used and could contribute, as it did for the post-doctoral student, a new dimension to information offerings in the field of European history. I came to believe that its use could attract faculty members and students in the field who may be unfamiliar with searching capabilities of online systems because there are few available.

FIGURE 10. Typical Entry from LBIBLIO File in STN

```
L2  ANSWER 1 OF 5
AN  (87)870263617  LBIBLIO
TI  The last Jews in Berlin <dt.>
    Versteckt: wie Juden in Berlin d. Nazi-Zeit *ueberlebten.
AU  Gross, Leonard
AS  Leonard Gross. Dt. von Cornelia Holfelder-v.d. Tann
PB  G*uetersloh : Bertelsmann-Club; Kornwestheim : EBG-Verl.-GmbH,
    [1986].
SO  379 S. ; 21 cm. - (nur f*uer Mitglieder). - Lizenzausg. d.
    Rowohlt-Verl., Reinbek.
DN  87,B10,0694
```

CONCLUSIONS

European databases of various kinds add a potentially new element to the mix of reference services available to scholars in the humanities and social sciences. But their implementation is not entirely without problems and may depend as much on the language and technical expertise of the searcher as on the contents of the database itself. In comparison to training for the use of English-language databases, in which group training is appropriate, application of these database may be dependent on an individualized approach that relies on personal skills, responsibilities, and determination.

REFERENCES

1. Olmsted, Marcia and Sylvie Labrèche. "DIALOG Version 2/QUESTEL PLUS: A Comparison." *Online*, 10, no. 1 (1986): 26-29; no. 2, 31-35; no. 3, 68-72.
2. Sweetland, James H. "America: History and Life – A Wide-Ranging Database." *Database*, 6, no. 4 (1983): 26.
3. Hensley, Colin. "European Community Databases: Online to Europe." *Database*, 11 (Dec. 1989): 45-52.
4. Hensley, p. 47.
5. *Directory of Public Databases Produced by the Commission of the European Communities*. Brussels: The Commission, 1989.
6. Wagers, Robert. "Can Easy Searching be Good Searching? A Model for Easy Searching." *Online*, 13, no. 2 (May, 1989): 84.
7. Large, J.A. "The Foreign-language Barrier and Electronic Information." *Online Review*, 14, no. 4 (Aug., 1990): 251-266.
8. Welsch, Erwin K. and Ellen Schultz. "Developing Gateways to Online information Utilities," *Library Software Review*, 9, no. 2 (March-April, 1990).

1992 and Beyond: In Conclusion

Maureen Pastine

In the Spirit of 1992: Access to Western European Libraries and Literature is on the growth and development of online access to bibliographic records. This work is intended to assist librarians and other educators in developing a broader world view, a more global perspective on the interconnectedness available through electronic information access, in this case, to Western European resources. It is crucial that librarians can ably interrogate the information infrastructure so vital to international growth and development, as well as to world understanding. This is one step in that direction.

Information technology is increasingly available in colleges and universities on both sides of the Atlantic. In Europe this cooperative networking effort is taking place through the initiatives of the Commission of the European Communities' (CEC) Plan of Action for Libraries in the European Community (EC).

The significant interest in Europe has fueled several other excellent sources of information resources on access to European library resources. Among the first is *Bibliographic Access in Europe: First International Conference* (Lorcan Dempsey, ed. Hants, England: Gower Publishing Company Ltd., 1990). *Bibliographic Access in Europe* is the proceedings of a conference organized by the Centre for Bibliographic Management and held at the University of Bath, September 14-17, 1989. In addition to this title and other books, articles, and documents mentioned by, or listed by, the authors of the chapters in this volume, a number of other publications will prove useful to those who would like to know more about the subject [see Appendix].

In addition a number of organizations can also provide extensive information on the state of online networking and other connections among libraries in Western Europe. These include the International Federation of Library Associations and Institutions (IFLA). IFLA's Standing Committee of the Section on Information Technology, the Universal Dataflow and Telecommunication (UDT) Core Program, has presented a study on electronic document delivery in Europe at the IFLA conference in Moscow in 1991. This group is working on multi-script and multi-lingual records and an expert system aid to automatic classification being carried out by OCLC. IFLA is involved in the development of user and graphic interfaces, Universal Bibliographic Control and International MARC (UBCIM), UDT, and Universal Availability of Publications (UAP).

There is also an European Foundation for Library Cooperation (EFLC) which was founded in 1985 and in 1986 was registered at The Hague in Lausanne. There are now nineteen members from among various scientific, economic, and political sectors in nine European countries. An EFLC initiative, a First European Conference on Library Automation and Networking was held on May 9-11, 1990. This gathering was intended to further the EFLC aim to strengthen library cooperation in Europe and thereby the management of libraries' information resources in order to further improve user services.

The Ligue Dis Bibliotheques Europeenes De Recherche (LIBER) is a nongovernment association of European research libraries. It was founded in 1971 under the auspices of the Council of Europe. It includes some 270 major libraries in 23 European countries. It publishes the *Directory of Library Networks in Europe*.

The European Library Automation Group (ELAG) convenes once a year providing a forum for 50 to 60 specialists in library automation from leading Western European library centers to the European Conference on Library Automation and Networking. The European Association for Health Information and Libraries (EAHIL) comprises nearly 500 individual, institutional, and collective members. These include health librarians and information specialists, institutions (medical schools, pharmaceutical industries, hospitals, other health services) and professional associations. Its aim is to contribute to its members' information, training, and representation at the international level, as well as to cooperation between health libraries and information services in Europe.

A proposed CEC Plan of Action for Libraries in the European Communities was presented to and endorsed by delegates of the member States. Specific action will include the new Framework Programme for Research and Technological Development. It proposes Action Lines which are targeted broadly at the development of machine-readable resources; interconnection of networks; the provision of new and enhanced services to users; the development of new Instructional Technology(IT) products for libraries; and the provision of training, transfer of skills experience and support.

The Essen University Library in Essen Germany also sponsors an annual symposium in October of each year related to some aspect of international library automation and networking. Attendance is limited to approximately 75-80 invited participants from Europe, Canada, and the United States.

EUSIDIC, the European Association of Information Services, began 20 years ago (1970) as a club of organizations interested in scientific and technical information. It now has 200 membership organizations.

SCIMP (Selective, Cooperative Indexing of Management Periodicals) set up by the European Business School Librarians Group (EBSLA) is another organization which indexes management literature in France, Germany, and the United Kingdom, and supplements this with coverage of America and other international journals in the field. It began indexing with the 1978-1986 time period and its database now has over 50,000 references. It adds to this some 6,000 items per year. Participating institutions are based in Sweden, Norway, Denmark, Finland, France, the Netherlands, Switzerland, Spain, Eire, and the United Kingdom. It scans 240 journals for its online index.

Beatrice Van Bockstaele, U.S. correspondent to the Automation and New Technology Department of the Bibliotheque de France (official name of the IGB) 412-687-0220, can be contacted about the Tres Grande Bibliotheque, the acronym for the new Bibliotheque Nationale being built in Paris. The Tres Grande Bibliotheque will be a high technology library. It will digitize old texts, creating an electronic library, with online books, films, videos, and telecommunications.

In addition to the these organizations working towards improved access to European library information access, OCLC plays a key role. Thirty percent of its database is European titles. There were 79 participating libraries in OCLC in Europe in 1988 and this number is growing even though coverage of bibliographic records in European libraries is still under fifty percent.

Through the Internet, a network based on the NSF (National Science Foundation) network, many of the European library databases are accessible. The Internet comprises a network of networks that provides global access to computing and information resources. Its connections to regional, government, and campus networks are also able to connect to international networks in North America, Latin America, Europe, and the Pacific Rim.

Another scholarly network in the United States which is of interest to librarians is BITNET. BITNET is used primarily for electronic mail, file transfers, and special interest group forums. Its communications capability is not as great as the Internet, but European and other librarians around the world can access BITNET. There is an excellent article on using "BITNET and the Internet: Scholarly Networks for Librarians," by William A. Britten, in *C & RL News* 51 (February 1990): 103-107.

There is, in the United States, an evolving national research network developing. A Coalition for Networked Information (CNI) supports this proposed National Research Education Network (NREN). This organization, CNI, is made up of administrators from over many institutions and organizations and continues to grow. It began with academic librarians and computer center directors and is expanding to all types of other libraries and information agencies. Sponsored by the Association of Research Libraries (ARL), CAUSE (Association for the Management of Information Technology in Higher Education), and EDUCOM, CNI was formed in March of 1990 to advance scholarship and intellectual productivity by promoting access to information resources through existing networks and the proposed NREN. Access to NREN will be crucial for exchanges between North American and Western European libraries in the future.

Euronet/DIANE Network was the first transnational packet-switched network in Europe. It supported public and private online information databases but Euronet was phased out in 1984. JANET

(Joint Academic Network) and other European networks abound [see Appendix].

The United States, Canada, the Netherlands and Norway lead the way in online control of library bibliographic records. In Europe, the plan is that national systems like PICA will continue and be interconnected with standard links much like the networks are connected in the United States.

An interlibrary loan venture connecting union catalogs in England, France, and the Netherlands is a pilot project supported by PICA with LASER in the United Kingdom and the Sous-Direction des Bibliotheques (SDB) of the French Ministry of Education. This project uses OSI and the International Organization for Standardization's new interlibrary loan search and retrieve protocols. A future project will experiment with electronic document exchange as part of the interlibrary loan work. In the Netherlands the computerized interlibrary loan facility was introduced in 1983, and it is used now by 250 libraries. The Pilot Demonstration Project for Interlending between library networks in Europe will communicate on the international level with the participants acting as gateways to the international infrastructure. It will help the participating libraries break down barriers that exist now.

It is anticipated that by the beginning of the next century there will be broad-based global connectivity. Libraries will negotiate contracts for access to other libraries' resources within and among countries while continuing to purchase a more limited number of books and subscriptions for local ownership. Copyright issues, leasing, licensing, and contract law issues will be of great importance in gaining access to the control of electronically formatted intellectual property.

European libraries, like American libraries are beginning to place far greater emphasis on certain aspects of electronic resource sharing that create problems, i.e., full text delivery and speedy/timely document delivery. Telefacsimile and the development of improved document transmission systems combined with a national telecommunications network (with links to international coverage) are already affecting improvements in methods of delivery. However, full-text information in electronic format is still quite limited. It is anticipated that this is an area that will grow in future years as text, multimedia, and graphics digitizing become more and more commonplace.

Interlibrary loan demands have increased everywhere with access to library catalogs on the Internet or at least more widely available in local or regional online networks. A major problem is that many libraries are not set up to deal with these increased pressures and the procedures in place are just not adequate to meet the increasing demands for resources and the increasing pressure to respond in a very brief time period to such demands. Libraries are not used to such a heavy emphasis on resource sharing. It is obvious that dramatic changes are going to be occurring in this more traditional arena. There are experiments taking place now where individuals can complete interlibrary loan forms online without going through intermediaries; and, in some cases an individual can order telefacsimile full text materials and pay for these online. These changes are transforming library services and operations throughout the world. OCLC is a leader in document transmission and telefacsimile systems and will undoubtedly play a crucial role in this for European libraries as well as within the United States.

Cooperation among libraries in Europe is crucial. There are great needs for models for cooperative funding and management, and for conversion of print to electronic form. As is true of all countries, Western European libraries are finding that the key element driving library development for the next decade and beyond is the public's need for information. But Europe has special needs not felt within the United States to the same extent that is demonstrated in a multilingual world. Much work remains to be done to be able to provide a multilingual catalog and multilingual access to bibliographic records in many languages, often using varying non-standardized paper bibliographic records. Networking is increasing nationally, but it is a slow process in Europe largely related to the language barriers and the need for standardization of end-user products, telecommunications links, communications protocols, and so forth.

The integrated-services digital network (ISDN) telecommunications systems will no doubt play a role in reducing some of the problems now inherent in sharing resources within Europe and throughout the world. ISDN provides a common user interface to digital networks all over the world. It is a system that provides voice, video, and high-speed data transmission through a single channel for long distance communication. It combines all communication services currently offered over separate networks into a single network to which any subscriber has access over common facilities through a single plug in the wall. It will bind the various communications and computing technologies into a coherent whole, connecting most major cities in the world within the next few years. It offers high speed telecommunications services and access to databases through local telephone systems.

Local area (LANs) and wide area (WANs) networks are springing up everywhere to interconnect microcomputers and large central storage sites and to permit the sharing of peripherals. These LANs are frequently equipped with gateways expanding into the public and private packet-switched networks for long-haul transmission. These too are being used in European libraries and will undoubtedly grow along with CD-ROM catalogs and databases.

Issues still to be resolved in access to European library resources include problems of inadequate retrospective conversion of paper records into machine readable records; lack of standardization in linkages; incompatible hardware and software; copyright problems; the economics of information; and governmental regulations and restrictions. There is also a need for a minimum of standardized information in the authority files of all the databases linked at the national and international level. There are many more barriers to ease of access to library resources in Europe including large backlogs of uncataloged items; problems related to multiple languages; differing copyright laws; differing methods of dissemination of government information; and differing ways of operating national telecommunications monopolies. Language barriers are a difficult problem to overcome even though some work is being done on advanced multilingual intelligent interfaces where endusers have access to different databases on a number of different hosts in a uniform way, using natural language.

A number of European projects are being worked on to facilitate international interconnection of systems for shared cataloging and interlibrary loan; to stimulate innovative library services based on new information technologies; and to stimulate exchange of systems and dissemination of knowledge to member states libraries.

One of the major difficulties impeding Europe-wide interconnection to libraries are the regional discrepancies. Other problems include human resources and budgetary constraints; prohibitive costs of international telecommunication tariffs, taxes, and postal rates; low total budget allocations for innovations and system implementation; inadequate funds for continuing education and training; inadequate funds for project preparation; technical incompatabilities; and most of the available funds going to the larger and better funded libraries. Another problem is incompatible internal library and information systems, duplication of work, and inadequate bibliographic control.

The lack of fully developed standards to support linkage of systems is a real problem. Standard communication protocols are foundations for effective networking. The work being done on an international basis by many different standards groups will help to resolve problems [see Appendix]. Standards like those for OSI and bibliographic data interchange format will assist cooperative projects such as the European register of microform masters, assist in record sharing from national bibliographies for cataloging purposes, and assist with interlibrary loan. It is doubtful if there will ever be one centralized European database of library holdings so standard linkages are crucial. Unlike library networks in North America, which tend to grow into very large systems, library networks in Europe are divided into small parts, representing a lot of regional and in some small countries even national networks.

There are European plans for achieving a degree of functional unity among the systems distributed throughout Europe. European cooperation is needed on many levels in the future, and technology should position itself to assist in end-user functions such as interlibrary loan and document delivery. There are limitations to remote access including that it is not always possible to gain access from the wide variety of terminals available; copyright and licensing agreements often restrict access to portions of online library systems to authorized users only; and catalogs provide intellectual access to bibliographic citations but not necessarily access to the physical items themselves.

The development of networks has created tremendous opportunities for library cooperation and a wide range of emerging information services. Typically these networks support file transfer, electronic mail, and interactive terminal access. The concept of a controlled number of decentralized sources of document supply supported by a comprehensive technological infrastructure seems to be part of the European Community plan.

Document transmission workstations are needed. These should be equipped with scanning devices and laser printers to convert documents to electronic form by means of scanners and subsequently stored and/or transmitted through the network in such a way that a requesting library could receive the requested document in electronic form on a workstation. End-users might even receive the documents in electronic form on their own workstations. Document transfer can only be a success if a large user-base of compatible workstations is installed in all countries of Europe and North America. Document transfer is necessary to establish cooperation with other networks and countries to create a compatible infrastructure, and this is only possible through the establishment of standards through the International Forum for Open Bibliographic Systems.

APPENDIX

Bibliography

Carpenter, Michael, ed. *National and International Bibliographic Databases: Trends and Prospects*. New York, The Haworth Press, Inc., 1988. (Cataloging & Classification Quarterly 8, no. 3/4 [1988]).
Centre for Bibliographic Management. *Library Bibliographic Networks in Europe: A LIBER Directory*. The Hague: NBLC, 1988.
Centre on Transnational Corporations. United Nations. *Transborder Data Flows: Access to the International On-Line Data-base Market*. North-Holland-Amsterdam, The Netherlands and New York, Oxford. New York: Elsevier, 1982.
Costers, L. "Interlibrary Loan Developments in the Netherlands," *Interlending and Document Supply*, 18 (1), 1990. pp. 8-11.
Costers, Look. "Planning an Experimental OSI-Network for Interlending in Europe," *Iatul (International Association of Technological University Libraries) Quarterly*. 4 (1), pp. 9-17.
Dempsey, Lorcan. *Libraries, Networks and OSI: A Review with a Report on North American Developments*. Bath, England: The Library, University of Bath, UK Office for Library Networking, 1991. 230 p.
DIANEGUIDE, a database on online databases and databanks available in Eu-

rope, and an online directory of information brokers currently active within the EC Member States.

Durieux, Baudouin. *Online Information in Europe*. Calne, England: EUSIDIC, 1989. 176 p.

European Conference on Library Automation and Networking. May 9-11, 1990. Brussels, Belgium. Proceedings by K.G. Saur in Munich, Dec. 1990.

Eusidic Database Guide 1989.

The European Online Information Survey (Carried out for Learned Information by the consultancy Information Automation Ltd.). A Questionnaire-based Survey of Online Users in Europe, 1989.

Gradley, Ellen and A. Hopkinson. *Exchanging Bibliographic Data: MARC and Other International Formats*. Ottawa and Chicago: Canadian Library Association and ALA, 1990. 329 p.

Karrenberg, Daniel and Anke Goos. *European R & D E-Mail Directory*. European Unix Systems Users Group, Buntingford, Herts, England, 1988.

Kranch, Douglas A. "The Development and Impact of a Global Information System," *Information Technology and Libraries* 8, no. 4 (December 1989): 87-90.

Moussis, Nicholad. *"Access to Europe": an Overview: the Subject, the Author and the Reader*. Rixensart, Belgium: Euroconfidentiel, 1991.

Neubauer, Karl W. and E.R. Dyer, eds. *European Library Networks*. Norwood, New Jersey: Ablex, 1990. 435 p.

1991 Directory of EEC: Information Sources. Rixensart, Belgium: Euroconfidentiel, 1991. 900 p.

OPACs and Beyond: Proceedings of a Joint Meeting of the British Library, DBMIST, and OCLC, August 17-18, 1988. Dublin, OH: OCLC Online Computer Library Center, 1989.

Pisani, Assunta, ed. *Euro-Librarianship: Shared Resources and Shared Responsibilities*. Cambridge, Massachusetts: Harvard University, 1991.

Quarterman, John S. *The Matrix: Computer Networks and Conference Systems Worldwide*. Bedfore, MA: Digital Press, 1990. 752 p.

Schur, Herbert. *Czechoslovakia*. London: British Library, 1990.

Stone, Peter. *Janet: A Report on Its Use for Libraries*. London: British Library, 1990. 138 p.

Tenopir, Carol. "Online Databases: Predicting the Future," *Library Journal*, October 1, 1991: 70-71.

Winton, Sandy R., ed. *Meeting the Challenge: Proceedings of the 76th Annual Conference of the Scottish Library Association*. Motherwell: SLA, 1990. 78 p.

Examples of Networks:

BIBNETT - Netherlands and Scandinavian countries
BLCMP and North Rhine Westphalian Network
DENET - Denmark
ECHO - CEC's host
LASER - UK

FUNET - Finland
LINNEA - Finland
NORDUNET - Nordic Countries
PICA - Netherlands
PORBASE - Portugal
SBN - Italy
SUNET - Sweden
SUNIST - France
SURFnet - the Netherlands
SURIS - Iceland
SWITCH - Switzerland
UKCURL (Consortium of University Research Libraries Project) using JANET-7 of most significant university libraries in Great Britain
UNINETT - Norway

Standards and Standards Organizations:

The following are some of those standards (and standards organizations) now being developed:

ASCII American Standard Codes for Information Interchange
CCITT - a standards body concerned with telecommunications
Common Command language
Eureka Project COSINE (Cooperation for Open Systems Interconnection Networking in Europe)
FTAM (the ISO file transfer standard)
FORMEX a customized version of SGML.
Information Retrieval Protocol
   (ANSI/NISO Z39.50)
National Information on Software and Services (NISS) project which will connect institutions of higher education in the United Kingdom
National Information Retrieval System (IR)
NISO National Information Standards Organization
NLC, RLG, OCLC, LC, BLDSC, and PICA — international Forum on Open Bibliographic Systems (IFOBS) charged with the establishment of bibliographic standards profiles will work mainly through ISO/TC46 in its standardization process, and it will seek liaison status with TC46.
OSI
Remote Database Access (RDA) Standard, ISO
SGML (Standard Generalized Markup Language), ISO.
TCP/IP

For Product Safety Concerns and Information please contact our EU
representative GPSR@taylorandfrancis.com
Taylor & Francis Verlag GmbH, Kaufingerstraße 24, 80331 München, Germany

www.ingramcontent.com/pod-product-compliance
Lightning Source LLC
Chambersburg PA
CBHW052131300426
44116CB00010B/1860